40 Short Walks in

HAMPSHIRE &
ISLE OF WIGHT

Produced by AA Publishing
© AA Media Limited 2011

Researched and written by
David Foster

Additional material and walks
by David Hancock (updated by David Foster
and Nick Channer)

Commissioning Editor: David Popey
Series Management: Sandy Draper
Series Design: Tracey Butler
Copy-editor: Ann Stonehouse
Proofreader: Pam Stagg
Picture Researcher: Carol Walker
Internal Repro and Image Manipulation:
Sarah Montgomery
Cartography provided by the Mapping
Services Department of AA Publishing
Production: Lorraine Taylor

Published by AA Publishing (a trading name
of AA Media Limited, whose registered office
is Fanum House, Basing View, Basingstoke,
Hampshire RG21 4EA; registered number
06112600)

  This product
includes mapping
data licensed from the Ordnance Survey®
with the permission of the Controller of
Her Majesty's Stationery Office. © Crown
Copyright 2011. All rights reserved.
Licence number 100021153.

A04616

978-0-7495-6903-7
978-0-7495-6915-0 (SS)

Colour separation by AA Digital

Printed by Oriental Press

Visit AA Publishing at theAA.com/shop

A CIP catalogue record for this book is
available from the British Library.

The contents of this book are believed
correct at the time of printing. Nevertheless,
the publishers cannot be held responsible
for any errors or omissions or for changes
in the details given in this book or for
the consequences of any reliance on the
information it provides. This does not affect
your statutory rights. We have tried to
ensure accuracy in this book, but things do
change and we would be grateful if readers
would advise us of any inaccuracies they
may encounter.

We have taken all reasonable steps to ensure
that these walks are safe and achievable
by walkers with a realistic level of fitness.
However, all outdoor activities involve a
degree of risk and the publishers accept
no responsibility for any injuries caused to
readers whilst following these walks. For
more advice on walking safely see page 144
The mileage range shown on the front cover
is for guidance only – some walks may be
less than or exceed these distances.

Some of the walks may appear in other AA
books and publications.

Picture credits
The Automobile Association would like
to thank the following photographers,
companies and picture libraries for their
assistance in the preparation of this book.

Abbreviations for the picture credits are as
follows – (t) top; (b) bottom; (c) centre; (l)
left; (r) right; (AA) AA World Travel Library.

3 AA/Andrew Newey; 7 AA/Derek Forss; 10
John Glover/Alamy; 20 AA/Michael Moody;
34 AA/Wyn Voysey; 38 AA/Michael Moody;
53 AA/James Tims; 60/61 AA/James Tims;
72 AA/Steve Day; 84 AA/Adam Burton;
100/101 AA/Adam Burton; 112 AA/Michael
Moody; 124 ian badley/Alamy; 140 AA/Simon
McBride.

Every effort has been made to trace the
copyright holders, and we apologise in
advance for any accidental errors. We would
be happy to apply the corrections in the
following edition of this publication.

Acknowledgements
With thanks to Wightlink Ferries

Opposite: The Needles, Isle of Wight

40 Short Walks in

HAMPSHIRE & ISLE OF WIGHT

Contents

Walk	Rating	Distance	Page

Rating

Each walk is rated for its relative difficulty compared to the other walks in this book. Walks marked ✚✚✚ are likely to be shorter and easier with little total ascent. The hardest walks are marked ✚✚✚

Walking in Safety

For advice and safety tips see page 144.

Introduction

Let's start with the bit you can't walk on. For although the Solent divides the Isle of Wight from neighbouring Hampshire, this iconic stretch of water is also a unifying theme for this book. Its shores form the backdrop to walks on both sides of the water, with tantalising and ever-changing views between the mainland and England's largest offshore island. Here you'll see a constant stream of shipping from utilitarian container vessels to luxury liners; and these same waters are also busy with yachts and other small craft, especially during the annual summer Cowes Week in August.

Step ashore, and you'll quickly discover why the two counties are so popular with walkers. Hampshire now has two National Parks, while more than half of the Isle of Wight is officially designated as an Area of Outstanding Natural Beauty. These are among England's finest landscapes – but there's also some delightful countryside beyond their boundaries.

The chalk streams of the Test and Itchen characterise much of central Hampshire. Both rivers are famous for their trout fishing, running through quiet valleys with thatched villages and country pubs. Perhaps less well known, the more easterly River Meon inhabits an intimate wooded valley that lends its name to the walking trail along the former Meon Valley Railway.

South Downs National Park

Much of the Meon Valley now lies within the South Downs National Park. Running east from St Catherine's Hill on the outskirts of Winchester, the National Park encompasses the chalk downland south of Petersfield, and the gentler wooded landscapes of the Western Weald as far north as Alice Holt Forest, near Farnham. Further west, the free-roaming ponies, wide purple heaths and wooded inclosures of the New Forest give this National Park its uniquely enduring appeal.

The Isle of Wight

Across the water, the Isle of Wight is southern England in miniature. The central chalk ridge pushes westwards to the Needles, giving unrivalled views across the Island and the mainland coast from Swanage to Selsey Bill. Arable farmland lies mainly to the south, with dairy pasture, woodland and low-lying creeks to the north. This is ideal country for walkers, who cross the Solent in their thousands every May for the UK's largest walking festival. Together, Hampshire and the Isle of Wight share a combined network of over 3,500 miles (5,632km) of rights of way.

Opposite: Rockbourne

Walking through these pages you'll discover Iron Age hill-forts and Roman villas, as well as Britain's second oldest lighthouse, dating from the 14th century. The walks will transport you to key moments in English history such as the Civil War and the Monmouth Rebellion, while evidence of more recent conflicts includes the Needles Battery and a Second World War airfield. An altogether different conflict was acted out in Richard Adams' classic fable *Watership Down*, which is the focus of your walk at Ecchinswell. Other literary locations include Gilbert White's Selborne, and the clifftop scenery beloved by Alfred, Lord Tennyson on the Isle of Wight.

Many of the walks also includes a nearby attraction, leading you to inspirational gardens, great houses and steam railways. Simpler pleasures include significant churches, the Isle of Wight's only surviving windmill and pottering across the River Hamble on a ferry with a 500-year pedigree. And, speaking of ferries, you'll find walks within easy reach of the ferry terminals at Lymington, Yarmouth, Portsmouth and Fishbourne – the perfect excuse for a day out on the other side of the Solent!

Using the Book

This collection of 40 walks is easy to use. Use the locator map, see opposite, to select your walk, then turn to the map and directions of your choice. The route of each walk is shown on a map and clear directions help you follow the walk. Each route is accompanied by background information about the walk and area.

INFORMATION PANELS

An information panel for each walk details the total distance, landscape, paths, parking, public toilets and any special conditions that apply, such as restricted access or level of dog friendliness. The minimum time suggested for the walk is for reasonably fit walkers and doesn't allow for stops.

ASCENT AND DIFFICULTY

An indication of the gradients you will encounter is shown by the rating ▲▲▲ (no steep slopes) to ▲▲▲ (several very steep slopes). Walks are also rated for difficulty. Walks marked ✚✚✚ are likely to be shorter and easier with little total ascent. The hardest walks are marked ✚✚✚.

MAPS AND START POINTS

There are 40 maps covering the walks. Some walks have a suggested option in the same area. Each walk has a suggested Ordnance Survey map. The start of each walk is given as a six-figure grid reference prefixed by two letters indicating which 100km square of the National Grid it refers to. You'll find more information on grid references on most Ordnance Survey maps.

CAR PARKING

Many of the car parks suggested are public, but occasionally you may find you have to park on the roadside or in a lay-by. Please be considerate when you leave your car, ensuring that access roads or gates are not blocked and that other vehicles can pass safely.

DOGS

We have tried to give dog owners useful advice about how dog friendly each walk is. Please respect other countryside users. Keep your dog under control, especially around livestock, and obey local bylaws and other dog control notices. Remember, it is against the law to let your dog foul in public areas, especially in villages and towns.

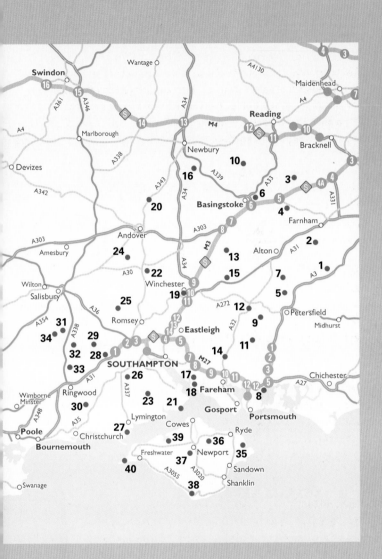

KEY TO WALKING MAPS

- - -→	Walk Route		Built-up Area
❶	Route Waypoint		Woodland Area
- - - -	Adjoining Path	🚻	Toilet
⚡	Viewpoint	🅿	Car Park
•	Place of Interest	🎪	Picnic Area
⌃	Steep Section	)(	Bridge

FOLLOWING FLORA'S FOOTSTEPS

Wild heathland contrasts with a wooded beauty spot in an area loved by Tennyson and the writer Flora Thompson.

Much of the landscape either side of the busy A3 in this peaceful corner of Hampshire is a mini wilderness of bracken and heather-covered commons and deep wooded valleys etched by tiny streams. Surprisingly, this unspoiled area was once the heart of a thriving iron industry, with streams like the Wey and Downwater being dammed to provide power for the great hammers in the 17th-century ironworks. Timber for the furnaces and iron ore were in plentiful supply locally.

Henry Hoake

The chain of dams and the lovely wooded ponds at Waggoner's Wells were created in 1615 by Henry Hooke, lord of the manor of Bramshott, to supply his iron foundry. Now a famous beauty spot owned by the National Trust, the three beautiful lakes, surrounded by splendid beech woods and home to a wealth of wildlife, are a delight to explore, especially during the autumn when the colours are magnificent.

Writers and Poets

Like the poet Tennyson and the writer Flora Thompson, who loved to stroll beside the pools, you will be immediately charmed by this secluded haven. Tennyson, who rented Grayshott Farm (now Grayshott Hall) in 1867, wrote his famous short ode 'Flower in the Crannied Wall' after pulling a flower from one of the crevices at the wishing well you will pass in the valley bottom.

Flora Thompson lived in both Liphook and Grayshott during her 30 years in Hampshire between 1897 and 1927. She often walked to Waggoner's Wells and Bramshott, returning to Grayshott via Ludshott Common. On these long, inspirational country rambles she would observe and assiduously make notes on the wildlife she encountered. Her detailed nature notes reflecting the changing year and written in semi-fictional style, appeared in her book *The Peverel Papers*. Flora also describes her life in the area and many of its inhabitants with great affection in the collection of essays called *Heatherley*, which was not published until 1979.

Opposite: Beech woodland canopy at Waggoner's Wells

Bramshott

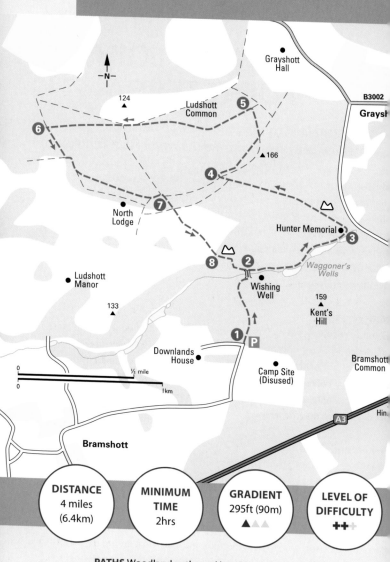

DISTANCE
4 miles
(6.4km)

MINIMUM
TIME
2hrs

GRADIENT
295ft (90m)
▲ ▲ ▲

LEVEL OF
DIFFICULTY
+++

PATHS Woodland paths and heathland tracks, 3 stiles
LANDSCAPE Wooded valley with lakes. Lofty, heather-covered common with far-
reaching views **SUGGESTED MAP** OS Explorer 133 Haslemere & Petersfield
START/FINISH Grid reference: SU 855336
DOG FRIENDLINESS Vast expanse of heathland where dogs can run free
PARKING Unsurfaced car park on edge of Bramshott Common
PUBLIC TOILETS None on route

WALK 1 DIRECTIONS

1 From the car park, take the defined path beyond the low barrier and gradually descend. At the bottom, take the main bridleway (marked by a blue arrow on a post) that directs you left along a sunken track. Ignore this if it's wet and muddy and climb the path ahead beneath beech trees, then at a fork, keep left down to reach the river and a footbridge.

2 Cross the bridge and turn right along the footpath parallel with the river. Pass the wishing well and a house and keep to the path through the valley bottom to the left of three ponds, eventually reaching a lane by a ford.

3 Just before the lane, turn sharp left, pass a memorial stone and steeply ascend through mixed woodland. As it levels out, cross a path, then a track and soon merge with a wide gravel track. Keep left, pass a bridleway on the left, then, where the track begins to curve left downhill, keep straight on along a path through trees.

4 Cross a path, then turn right after 50yds (46m) at a broad sandy track bordering lightly wooded heathland. On reaching a junction, fork left across the common. The path soon widens and descends to a T-junction.

5 Turn left and follow this heathland trail, edged by bracken and gorse and

> ### 🍴 EATING AND DRINKING
> There are no refreshments available on the route but it makes for an ideal morning, afternoon or summer's evening walk, so why not enjoy a picnic beside one of the three delightful ponds at Waggoner's Wells.

eventually merge with a wider sandy trail. Keep left then, on reaching a bench and junction of ways on the common fringe, proceed straight on through the conifer plantation.

6 At a crossing of paths by a line of electricity poles, turn left with bridleway signs. Bear gently right at a crossways, following the bridleway close to the woodland fringe. Turn left beside electricity poles and ignore a bridleway turning right. Bear left with the poles; then, after 100yds (91m) turn right at a crossways and broken bridleway sign.

7 Turn right and keep straight on at the next crossing of routes, following the footpath marker alongside a garden to a stile on the woodland edge. Keep ahead between wire fences to a stile in the field corner.

8 Steeply descend into woodland to reach a stile. At the track beyond, turn right downhill to the river and footbridge encountered on the outward route. Retrace your steps back to the car park.

WAR AND PEACE IN THE WOODS

Follow the beautiful Lodge Pond Trail
around this popular and historic woodland.

There's been a forest at Alice Holt since about 5000 BC. Iron Age people were using the local clay, water and fuel to make pottery here in the 1st century BC and those potteries expanded into a major industry in the years following the Roman invasion.

Many of the trees had already been felled to fuel the pottery kilns by the time the Romans left, early in the 5th century. The Saxons continued the felling, this time to create fields for their crops but by the Middle Ages Alice Holt had become a royal hunting forest governed by a strict legal code. In later centuries more timber was extracted for construction and shipbuilding, so that by 1655 Charles II ordered the woods to be replanted. The forest's heartbeat is measured in decades and the trees grew quietly for more than 100 years until the Napoleonic Wars once again created a demand for shipbuilding timber.

Replanting a Forest

The modern history of Alice Holt really began after the Enclosure Act of 1812, when 1,600 acres (648ha) were enclosed and once again replanted with oak. By the time those trees came to maturity Britain was in the thick of the First World War and the coal mines and trenches were swallowing up vast quantities of timber for pit props and revetments. Timber was a scarce commodity in post-war Britain and the government set up the Forestry Commission to help boost the supply of home-grown timber.

The new agency took over responsibility for Alice Holt in 1924 and set about planting quick growing conifers to meet the demand. Following the Second World War, the Commission began developing a research station around Alice Holt Lodge to the west of the A325 and additional laboratories were built in the late 1970s. Today, the Commission's scientists are working on topical issues like environmental change, as well as exploring potential sources of biomass energy.

But as you'll see from the picnic areas, play structures and recreation facilities on this walk have now become a major feature in some woodlands.

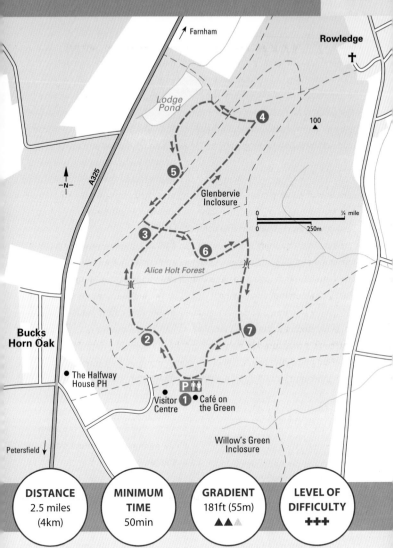

↑ Farnham

Rowledge ✝

Lodge Pond

④

100 ▲

⑤

Glenbervie Inclosure

A325

← N →

③

⑥

Alice Holt Forest

Bucks Horn Oak

② ⑦

• The Halfway House PH

Ⓟ ⛨
Visitor Centre ① Café on the Green

↓ Petersfield

Willow's Green Inclosure

0 ¼ mile
0 250m

DISTANCE	MINIMUM TIME	GRADIENT	LEVEL OF DIFFICULTY
2.5 miles (4km)	50min	181ft (55m) ▲▲▲	+++

PATHS Tracks and woodland paths, muddy in places, several flights of steps

LANDSCAPE Conifer woodland with some deciduous planting

SUGGESTED MAP OS Explorer 145 Guildford & Farnham,
Godalming & Farnborough **START/FINISH** Grid reference: SU 417813

DOG FRIENDLINESS Popular for dogs

PARKING Oak car park (pay-and-display)

PUBLIC TOILETS At the start

WALK 2 DIRECTIONS

1 Walk through the car park from the Education Centre and turn left at the blue waymark post opposite the large central signpost. Keep ahead past the turning on your left and follow the woodland path to a forest track.

2 Turn left for 45yds (41m) then turn right down the steps, cross a brook and climb the steps on the other side. Follow the winding trail past a bench seat and down the steps to cross a stream. Bear left beyond the steps on the other side, climbing steadily before the path levels out to a crossways.

3 Keep ahead, pass through a clearing and climb steadily to a blue waymark post a few paces before a narrow woodland path turns off to your left.

4 Turn left here, continue past a wooden barrier and turn left at the T-junction. Continue to a 5-way junction and keep ahead across the broad forest track, waymarked towards Lodge Pond. Keep ahead at the next junction and turn left to walk parallel with the edge of the pond. Bear left past the picnic tables, then turn right through a small parking area to a T-junction.

5 Turn right onto the forest track and continue for 500yds (457m) to a waymarked crossways. Turn left, keep ahead at the crossways that you passed earlier (Point **3**), then take the right-hand turning onto a narrow path that leads down to a large play structure.

6 Turn left, pass the picnic table and two more play structures, then turn right at the crossways. Cross a stream, keep ahead at the Giants Play Area, then climb almost to the summit of the hill.

7 Turn right, pass another play area, turn left, then right past more play equipment to reach the forest centre. Turn right past the Café on the Green and walk back to the car park.

> ### 🐾 ON THE WALK
> The woodlands at Alice Holt are managed for their wildlife. You might see birds like the lesser spotted woodpecker, nightjar or willow tit, as well as the purple emperor butterfly, which is the emblem of Alice Holt Forest. Perhaps more obviously, large mammals including muntjac and roe deer live in the woods.

> ### 🍽 EATING AND DRINKING
> The log cabin-style Café on the Green is right next to the car park and opens daily for drinks, ice creams and hot and cold food to eat in or take away. Expect sandwiches, paninis, all-day breakfast, home-made soup and jacket potatoes. Alternatively, the Halfway House is a cosy little stone-built pub just around the corner on the A325.

RAGS TO RICHES AT ELVETHAM

A walk through time and social class on the outskirts of a thriving Hampshire village.

Today, golf is a relatively genteel pastime – but, as you walk out across Hartley Wintney golf course, spare a thought for those who came here before you. For this was the site of the early 19th-century workhouse that served Hartley Wintney and a dozen of the surrounding parishes. Opened in the spring of 1835, the building was enlarged in the following year and stood here until a new workhouse was constructed at nearby Winchfield in 1871.

Yet just 0.5 miles (800m) from the grinding poverty of the old workhouse stands a building of a different order. From the 15th century, Elvetham Hall was home to the family of Jane Seymour, the third wife of Henry VIII. Henry visited the house at least twice in the 1530s and in 1591 Edward Seymour, Earl of Hertford, entertained Queen Elizabeth I at Elvetham for four days. Her entourage stayed in specially-built pavilions close to the house and the queen planted an oak tree to commemorate her visit.

After Edward died, his grandson William Seymour, the Marquis of Hertford and Duke of Somerset, inherited the Elvetham Estate. William sold the house in 1649 and after a complex series of marriages the property passed into the hands of the Gough-Calthorpe family. The great building stood for another two centuries until it was destroyed by a major fire in 1840.

A Victorian Phoenix

Enter Frederick Gough, the 4th Baron Calthorpe. He commissioned Samuel Teulon to design the magnificent Victorian Gothic mansion and stables block that rose from the ashes of the old house in 1860. Teulon's building is now home to the sumptuous Elvetham Hotel and you'll have glimpses of the mansion's spectacular roofline soon after leaving the golf course.

The hotel stands in 35 acres (14ha) of grounds, with formal gardens, croquet lawn and a broad yew tree walk. It's said to have the largest magnolia *soulangiana* in England and Queen Elizabeth's oak tree, which is now over 32 feet (9.8m) in circumference, still stands in the hotel grounds. If you'd like to get a closer look at the building, the hotel restaurant is open for Sunday lunch throughout the year.

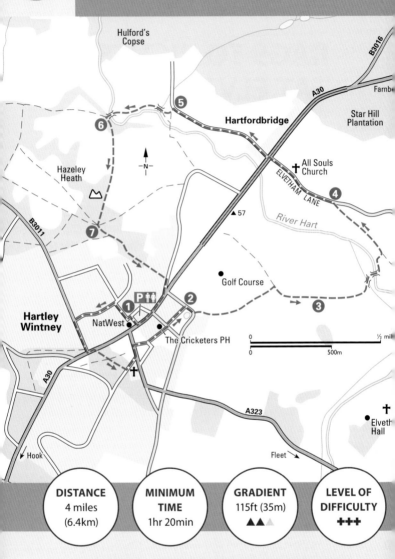

Hulford's Copse

B3016

Hartfordbridge

A30

Farnb

Star Hill Plantation

All Souls Church

ELVETHAM LANE

Hazeley Heath

River Hart

▲ 57

B3011

Hartley Wintney

Golf Course

NatWest

The Cricketers PH

A30

A323

Elveth Hall

↙ Hook

Fleet →

0   ½ mil
0   500m

DISTANCE	MINIMUM TIME	GRADIENT	LEVEL OF DIFFICULTY
4 miles (6.4km)	1hr 20min	115ft (35m) ▲▲▲	+++

PATHS Field paths, minor roads and woodland tracks, 7 stiles
LANDSCAPE Golf course, wooded farmland and heath
SUGGESTED MAP OS Explorer 144 Basingstoke, Alton & Whitchurch
START/FINISH Grid reference: SU 766569
DOG FRIENDLINESS Can run free on Hazeley Heath
PARKING Monachus Lane car park (pay-and-display)
PUBLIC TOILETS At the start

WALK 3 DIRECTIONS

1 Leave the car park by the vehicle exit, walk up Walpole Gardens and turn left along Hartford Road. Turn left at the T-junction, cross the A30, then zig-zag left and right onto the narrow surfaced path to the church of St John the Evangelist. Turn left, cross the A323 at the lights and walk across the green past the Cricketers pub.

2 Turn right up Park Corner Road to the pond, then turn left over a squeeze stile onto the signposted path that winds around the edge of golf course. Pass the reed-fringed pond and keep ahead over the stile out of the golf course.

🍴 EATING AND DRINKING

Standing opposite the cricket field near the start of your walk, the Cricketers offers a good choice of wines and real ales to accompany filled ciabattas, baguettes and sandwiches. There's also a full French restaurant menu. Alternatively, try the Little House Tea Room in the High Street for breakfast, light lunches and cream teas.

3 Walk along the right-hand edge of the field, go through the gap in the far corner and then continue over the footbridge and along the enclosed path to a stile. Turn left along the green lane to a stile and keep ahead across the open field to a stile beside the right-hand gate in the far hedge.

4 Turn left along Elvetham Lane to the A30 at Hartfordbridge. Cross over and keep ahead up the 'no through road' until it bends sharp right.

5 Keep ahead through the kissing gate and follow the waymarked route through the paddocks to a pair of gates and plank bridge. Continue through a kissing gate and along the enclosed path, go through another kissing gate and keep ahead across the grassy clearing to a footbridge.

🌳 IN THE AREA

Just 1 mile (1.6km) from Hartley Witney, West Green House gardens are a blend of formal box hedges and borders, as well as lakes and follies. They were laid out by Marilyn Abbott, after she leased the gardens from the National Trust in 1993. The gardens are open from April to September.

6 Cross over, turn left and follow the woodland path over a series of plank bridges leading out along the edge of Hazeley Heath. Climb steeply to a summit, enter the trees and bear right until you reach a firm, wide track.

7 Turn left, ignore all turnings and drop down through the trees to a kissing gate. Keep ahead past the houses onto the narrow path that leads out onto Hunts Common, opposite Hartley Wintney Golf Club. Turn right into the High Street, then right again before NatWest Bank to the car park.

ODIHAM AND THE BASINGSTOKE CANAL

Combine the elegant little town of Odiham with the leafy Basingstoke Canal.

Flanked by the expanding towns of Aldershot and Basingstoke, Odiham retains an unspoiled, country-town atmosphere. Handsome Georgian houses and colour-washed, timber-framed cottages line the wide main street, making this one of Hampshire's most elegant small towns. Right in the centre you'll pass the George Hotel, which was first licensed in 1540. Other highlights, including the 14th-century church, Tudor vicarage and the Bury with its stocks and whipping-post, lie just a few paces off your route.

Canal Link to London

Away from the town, you'll follow the Basingstoke Canal from Odiham Wharf, which once saw shipments of timber, grain, coal and manufactured goods. When the canal opened in 1794, the route included 29 locks, 69 bridges, two aqueducts and – significantly – the 1,230yd (1,125m) tunnel at Greywell. Traffic was brisk during the Napoleonic Wars, which disrupted shipping in the English Channel but the coming of the railways in the 1840s led to its gradual decline. Nevertheless, the canal was used to transport materials for the construction of Aldershot Garrison in the 1850s and it was later requisitioned for shifting munitions during the First World War. But the canal company's finances were never in good shape and the waterway was sold several times in the late 19th and early 20th centuries.

The Canal Today

Greywell Tunnel collapsed in 1932, severing the link with Basingstoke and hastening the canal's demise. Sections were sold off and, by the 1960s, the canal had become almost totally derelict. The restored canal re-opened in 1991 and now forms one of Britain's finest areas for aquatic plants. Surprisingly though, the canal is more famous for its nightlife. The disused Greywell Tunnel is now home to 12,500 bats of all native species, including Natterer's and Daubenton's and is the largest bat roost in Britain. At dusk, visitors to the tunnel entrance, close to the Fox and Goose pub in Greywell, can witness the spectacle of thousands of bats leaving the tunnel to feed.

Opposite: Boats for hire along the Basingstoke Canal at Odiham

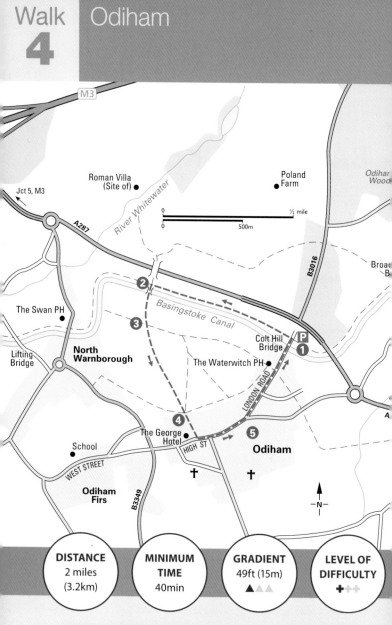

DISTANCE
2 miles
(3.2km)

MINIMUM TIME
40min

GRADIENT
49ft (15m)
▲▲▲

LEVEL OF DIFFICULTY
✚✚✚

PATHS Canal tow path, field paths and town centre pavements, 1 stile
LANDSCAPE Canal, farmland and Georgian town centre
SUGGESTED MAP OS Explorer 144 Basingstoke, Alton & Whitchurch
START/FINISH Grid reference: SU 747516
DOG FRIENDLINESS Leads required in grazing fields and town
PARKING Odiham Wharf car park, London Road
PUBLIC TOILETS None on route

WALK 4 DIRECTIONS

❶ Take the short gravelled path from the car park to the canal, turn right along the tow path under Colt Hill Bridge and follow canal for almost 0.75 miles (1km).

❷ Cross the canal at the first bridge, nip over the stile and follow the right-hand field-edge to the kissing gate in the far corner.

❸ Bear gently left across the next field, cross the plank bridge at a gap in the hedge and walk across another field, heading a little to the left of the church tower. Dodge through the gap in the

> **🦢 ON THE WALK**
> Dragonflies and butterflies abound and the tow path is a good place for birding. You may see mallards, wagtails, herons and little grebes, as well as summer migrants like spotted flycatcher, willow warbler and swallows skimming low over the water. If you're lucky, you might even spot the blue flash of the kingfisher.

corner of the field and continue on the same heading to the left-hand of two kissing gates in the far hedge.

❹ Walk through the passage between the buildings to reach Odiham High Street beside the George Hotel. Turn left and follow the High Street as far as the junction with London Road.

❺ Fork left and walk down London Road past the Waterwitch pub. Finally, cross Colt Hill Bridge, turn right and follow the path to the car park.

> **🍴 EATING AND DRINKING**
> Odiham has a good range of pubs, restaurants and bistros, as well as a couple of tea rooms. Right at the end of your walk, the Waterwitch pub offers real ales and an extensive all-day bar menu that ranges from sandwiches and jacket potatoes to pub favourites and grills. There are welcoming log fires in winter and a large canalside garden.

> **🌿 IN THE AREA**
> Stroll around Odiham. Behind All Saints Church and close to the 17th-century almshouses you'll find the pest house, built at about the same time to isolate suspected sufferers of the plague. This fine example is one of only a few that survive in Hampshire today; it was converted to a private house in 1780 and is now a museum. The graves of several French prisoners lie in the churchyard; they were held at a camp in an old chalk pit on the Alton road during the Napoleonic War and are believed to have helped build the Basingstoke Canal.

LOOKING FOR EDWARD THOMAS

Explore the beech-clad hills and vales
that so inspired Hampshire's great poet.

William Cobbett wrote 'beautiful beyond description' in his *Rural Rides*, after passing through Hawkley in 1822, on his way from East Meon to Thursley. In common with other famous literary people who once lived in and wrote about this area, such as naturalist Gilbert White (see Walk 7) and poet Edward Thomas, Cobbett was enchanted by the rolling, beech-clad hills that characterise this relatively unexplored part of Hampshire.

Abiding Love

Known locally as 'hangers', from the Anglo-Saxon 'hangra' meaning 'sloping wood', these fine beech woods cling to the steep chalk escarpment that links Selborne to Steep. Many have charming names such as Happersnapper Hanger and Strawberry Hanger. Edward Thomas lived at Steep from 1906 to his death in the First World War in 1917. His abiding love for the beech hangers, mysterious combes and the sheer beauty of the landscape inspired him to write some of his finest poems, including Up in the Wind, The New House and Wind and Mist. You, too, will find the views breathtaking as you dip and climb through the hangers to the summit of Shoulder of Mutton Hill, Thomas's favoured spot above his beloved Steep.

Along the Route

The walk begins from Hawkley, tucked away beneath Hawkley Hanger. Resisting the temptations to be found at the Hawkley Inn, you descend into the lush meadows of the Oakshott Valley, before a steep ascent on an old droving track to the top of Shoulder of Mutton Hill. Here, in a tranquil glade on its higher slopes, you will find a sarsen stone dedicated to Edward Thomas. With such surprising views across Steep and of 'sixty miles of South Downs at one glance', as Thomas described it, it is no wonder that he loved this area.

The return walk joins the Hangers Way, a 21-mile (34km) long distance trail traversing East Hampshire from Queen Elizabeth Country Park to Alton. Following a steep descent through a meadow, carpeted with cowslips in spring, you follow the Oakshott Stream back to Hawkley.

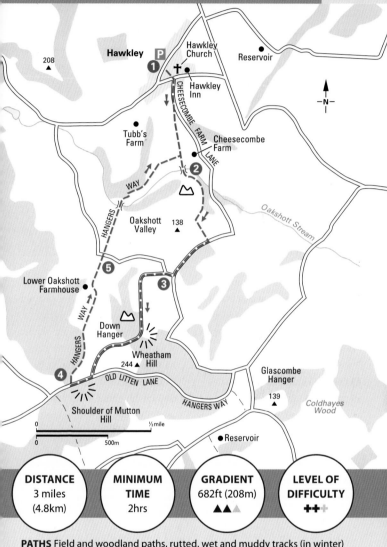

DISTANCE	MINIMUM TIME	GRADIENT	LEVEL OF DIFFICULTY
3 miles (4.8km)	2hrs	682ft (208m) ▲▲▲	╋╋╋

PATHS Field and woodland paths, rutted, wet and muddy tracks (in winter) and short stretches of road, 21 stiles **LANDSCAPE** Rolling, beech-clad hills, a hidden, flower-filled valley and undulating farmland

SUGGESTED MAP OS Explorer 133 Haslemere & Petersfield

START/FINISH Grid reference: SU 746291

DOG FRIENDLINESS Dogs to be kept under control at all times

PARKING By village green and church in Hawkley

PUBLIC TOILETS None; outdoor toilets opposite Harrow Inn accessible

WALK 5 DIRECTIONS

❶ With your back to Hawkley church, walk left beside the green to the road junction. With the Hawkley Inn away to your left, cross over and go down Cheesecombe Farm Lane, signed 'Hangers Way'. Shortly, bear right along a concrete path. Descend past a broken stile and keep on at the fork of paths, with Cheesecombe Farm to the left.

❷ Cross Oakshott Stream and keep left along the field-edge beside woodland. Steeply ascend to a stile, keep right to a further stile, then turn left beside the fence and drop down to a track. Turn right, to reach a lane, then right again for 55yds (50m) to take the waymarked right of way beside Wheatham Hill House.

❸ Climb the long and steep, chalky track up through Down Hanger (this gets very wet and muddy), with views east along the South Downs unfolding. At the top of Wheatham Hill, turn right at a T-junction of tracks along Old Litten Lane. In 300yds (274m), take the Hangers Way right over a stile. For the Edward Thomas memorial stone, continue along the track for 200yds (183m) and turn left with a waymarker. Pass beside the wooden barrier and drop down to the clearing on Shoulder of Mutton Hill.

> ### ℒ ON THE WALK
> Two memorials in All Saints Church at Steep are worth looking for. One is to Basil Marden who was killed in an avalanche in the Andes in 1928; the other is to a Martha Legg who died in 1829 at the remarkable age of 105.

❹ Follow the Hangers Way as it descends through the edge of beech woods and steeply down across meadowland, eventually joining the drive to Lower Oakshott Farmhouse and a road.

❺ Turn right, then left over the stile and follow the defined Hangers Way path through the Oakshott Valley, crossing stiles, plank bridges and meadows to the junction of paths before Cheesecombe Farm. Turn left to the stile and retrace your steps all the way back to Hawkley and your car.

> ### 🍽 EATING AND DRINKING
> Time your walk to coincide with lunch at the delightfully unspoiled, 16th-century Harrow Inn (credit cards not accepted) at nearby Steep. There are two characterful rooms with scrubbed wooden tables and warming winter fires. Expect ale straight from the cask, hearty soup and sandwiches and a cottage garden for summer imbibing. The equally rustic Hawkley Inn offers a warm welcome to walkers, microbrewery ales and imaginative home-cooked food.

TURBULENT TIMES AT BASING HOUSE

Relive scenes from the English Civil War
as you circle these impressive Tudor ruins.

Huddled around the ruins of Basing House, Old Basing is a miniature time capsule in the shadow of modern Basingstoke. As you stroll across the common or walk beside the picturesque River Loddon, it's hard to believe that you're little more than a mile (1.6km)from the bright new shopping malls, bars and cafés at Festival Place.

The modestly named Basing House was, in fact, a Tudor palace and in their time both Henry VIII and Elizabeth I came to stay. Built in 1535 on the site of a Norman castle, its 360 rooms made Basing the largest private house in England. This vast mansion was the home of Sir William Paulet, the first Marquis of Winchester and Lord Treasurer of England.

The Battle for Basing House

By the outbreak of the Civil War in 1642 Basing House was in the hands of the Royalist fifth Marquis of Winchester, John Paulet. Troops sheltered here after the Battle of Cheriton in 1644, making this iconic Royalist stronghold a natural target for the Parliamentarians. They attacked the house on no less than three occasions but the end came in October 1645 when, after a two-month siege, a Parliamentary battery under Oliver Cromwell's personal command finally breached Paulet's defences. As many as 100 people were reported killed in the attack, though some sources claim less than half that number. What's more certain is that Cromwell's troops went on to ransack the house and, following a major fire, Parliament ordered its destruction. It was never rebuilt.

John Paulet himself was charged with high treason, stripped of his estates and imprisoned in the Tower of London. Yet, in the end, Paulet escaped more lightly than his house. The charges against him were dropped and after the Restoration in 1660 Charles II gave him back the site of his former home.

You'll see the remains of this once majestic building from several angles as your walk completely encircles the site. The great banks of the original Norman castle are clearly visible, framed by fractured sections of Tudor brickwork. As you follow the riverside footpath, look out for the huge Tudor tithe barn on your right, one of the largest of its kind in England.

DISTANCE
1.5 miles
(2.4km)

MINIMUM TIME
40min

GRADIENT
82ft (25m)
▲▲▲

LEVEL OF DIFFICULTY
✚✚✚

PATHS Grass and gravel paths with stretches of minor road, 2 stiles
LANDSCAPE Grazing fields, village and riverside walk
SUGGESTED MAP OS Explorer 144 Basingstoke, Alton & Whitchurch
START/FINISH Grid reference: SU 655522
DOG FRIENDLINESS Lead required around village lanes and livestock
on the common **PARKING** Basingstoke Lime Pits car park (north)
PUBLIC TOILETS None on route

隐

WALK 6 DIRECTIONS

❶ Go through the kissing gate near to the road entrance and follow the grassy path to a second gate. Bear left onto the waymarked Basing Trail and follow the hedge on your left around the lower slopes of Basingstoke Common as far as the two small trees beside the trail information board.

❷ Cross the stile, then zig-zag left and right over the old canal bridge and follow Redbridge Lane to the junction with Basing Road. Turn left along the pavement for 100yds (91m), then turn sharp right onto the riverside footpath towards Basing House. Keep ahead to the trail information board just before the railway bridge.

🐾 ON THE WALK
The early part of your walk runs close to the abandoned section of the Basingstoke Canal and you'll cross it as you leave the common at Red Bridge. The canal earthworks are still visible in the grounds of Basing House, with other minor clues near the church. Finally, you'll cross the route once again near the Royal British Legion clubhouse.

❸ Turn right along the path beside the railway and bear right down a road to reach St Mary's Church. Cross the road and keep ahead through the churchyard with the church on your left. Turn right out of the gate and walk down the road for 150yds (137m) to the bend at Whytegates.

🍴 EATING AND DRINKING
The Millstone lies just beyond the railway bridge half-way round your walk. Wadworth's ales complement the straightforward menu of sandwiches and ploughman's, as well as hot dishes and vegetarian options. Portions are substantial and the meals are nicely presented; expect log fires in winter, or eat on the riverside patio when the sun's out.

❹ Turn left down the path beside the graveyard; turn left at the T-junction and walk out to the road opposite Old Basing Royal British Legion. Cross the road, walk through the car park and re-join the Basing Trail at a kissing gate. Continue through a gate and beside the Basing House boundary fence until it turns away to the right.

❺ Go across the common towards the woods bordering the A30. Bear right through a gap in the hedge that bisects the common and head for poplar trees on the horizon. Cross the stile to the right of the trees and down through the amphitheatre back to the car park.

🌿 IN THE AREA
Allow some extra time to visit Basing House and its Great Barn, built in 1535. Browse the displays or stop for a coffee in the visitor centre, stroll in the neat formal gardens and explore the house's remarkable story with the help of an audio tour. The site is open March to October.

IN THE FOOTSTEPS OF GILBERT WHITE

Through the glorious beech hangers and tranquil meadows that so inspired the eminent naturalist Gilbert White.

Selborne and its beautiful surrounding countryside, was made famous over two centuries ago by the writings and reputation of the clergyman and pioneer naturalist Gilbert White. Based on 40 years of observation and meticulous recording of the flora and fauna around the village, Gilbert White wrote *The Natural History and Antiquities of Selborne* in 1789.

Born in the village in 1720, White was the grandson of a vicar of Selborne and, having been ordained after attending Oxford, he returned to live in the village to serve as a curate at neighbouring parishes and at Selborne in 1751. From the age of ten until his death in 1793 he lived at The Wakes, a large rambling house that overlooks the village green (the Plestor) and church. Although the village has changed, White would find the surrounding landscape largely unspoiled and now preserved by the National Trust.

Up the Zig-Zag Path

The walk begins with a long ascent to the top of Selborne Hill and Common, a task made easier by the hard work put in by Gilbert White and his brother John in 1753, when they constructed the famous Zig-Zag path up the steep scarp face. White described the Common as 'a vast hill of chalk, rising three hundred feet above the village; and is divided into a sheep down, the high wood and a long hanging wood called The Hanger'. You are rewarded with peace and tranquillity when you reach White's Wishing Stone and magnificent views over the village. You can explore the maze of paths that criss-cross the Common but the main route threads through the glorious beech hangers to White's favourite viewpoint. Here White would pause to absorb the breathtaking cameo that took in his home, the church and the serene wooded landscape.

Back in the village, locate White's grave in the churchyard and visit St Mary's Church. Here you will find White's fine memorial window depicting St Francis of Assisi preaching to 82 birds, all of which are mentioned in his book. The second loop heads east through the Oakhanger Valley, following the Hangers Way to Priory Farm, the site of Selborne Priory.

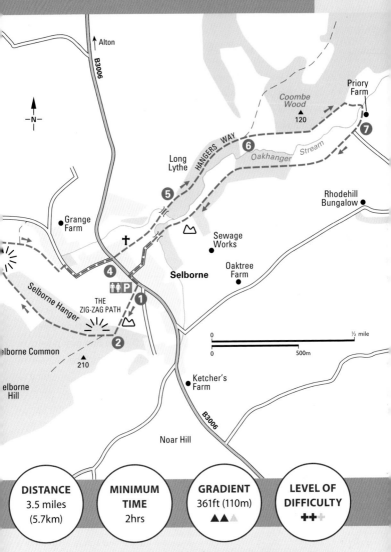

WALK 7 DIRECTIONS

❶ Take the arrowed footpath, signed 'The zig-zag and Hanger', by the car park entrance and gently ascend to a gate at the base of Selborne Common. Bear left to follow the impressive Zig-Zag path uphill, pausing at regular intervals to admire the unfolding view across the village.

❷ At the top, take the stepped path right and, in a few paces, keep right at a fork to follow the lower path through the beech hangers. Shortly, look out for a metal bench, by a path ascending from the right and savour the splendid view of the church and The Wakes through the gap in the trees. Continue along the main path, gently descending to a junction of paths, by a National Trust sign.

❸ Turn right downhill along a track then, where this curves left, bear off right across a stile into pasture. Keep to the left-hand edge, cross two more stiles and follow the enclosed path to a lane. Turn right and follow it back into the village, opposite the church.

> ## ⑪ EATING AND DRINKING
> Delicious light lunches, cakes and afternoon teas can be enjoyed in the civilised Tea Parlour at The Wakes, Gilbert White's house. Alternatively, try one of the two pubs, The Selborne Arms, which has a family room, or the Queens Inn for home-cooked bar food.

Turn right along the B3006 road for The Wakes and the car park, if you wish to cut the walk short.

❹ Cross the B road and follow the Hangers Way sign through the churchyard to a gate. Follow the defined path to a footbridge over the Oakhanger Stream.

❺ Keep to the Hangers Way through a gate and along the edge of meadowland to a gate, then pass through a stretch of woodland to a kissing gate and fork of paths.

❻ Proceed straight ahead (yellow arrow), leaving the Hangers Way. Eventually pass alongside a fence to a stile on the edge of Coombe Wood. Keep close to the woodland fringe to a stile, then bear left along the field-edge to a stile and turn right along a bridleway towards Priory Farm. Keep to the track through the farmyard to the metalled drive.

❼ In a few paces, where the drive curves left, bear off right along a track beside a bungalow. Go through a gate and follow the grassy track uphill along the field-edge, through a gate, eventually reaching a gate and woodland. Follow the track (can be muddy) through beech woodland. Leave the wood, passing a house called Dorton's and climb the lane steeply back to Selborne, turning left for the car park.

WILDLIFE ON THE DOORSTEP

Birds and bombs make a colourful backdrop to this bracing walk in Langstone Harbour.

Farlington Marshes, just across the Broom Channel from Portsea Island and the teeming city centre, are right in Portsmouth's back garden. Cut off from the north by the busy A27 and surrounded on three sides by Langstone Harbour, this peaceful wildlife reserve has been managed by the Hampshire and Isle of Wight Wildlife Trust since 1962.

Today these low-lying fields are internationally important for wildlife. The grassland areas are bright with butterflies and summer wild flowers, which include rarities such as sea barley, bulbous foxtail and slender hare's-ear. Summer is also the time to see breeding lapwing and skylark, while in winter the fields offer grazing and shelter to thousands of Brent geese. Other birds to look out for in and around the lagoons and reedbeds include bearded tits, wigeon, teal and black-tailed godwits.

But the site also has a fascinating history. The marshes as you'll see them now were created in the late 18th century, when the Lord of the Manor of Farlington reclaimed them from Langstone Harbour by linking some of the islands with a clay and timber wall. From that time onwards the marshes have provided rich grazing meadows and cattle were once raised here.

Wartime Deception

This pastoral idyll was rudely disturbed during the Second World War, when the War Department established an anti-aircraft battery on the site. The marshes were also used as a decoy to draw enemy bombers away from Portsmouth after the punishing raid in January 1941. Fires were lit in specially constructed bunkers, tricking the German pilots into bombing the still waters of Langstone Harbour instead of the blacked-out city centre. Look out for a couple of wartime brick structures as you walk around the harbour wall, as well as some small, round ponds formed in old bomb craters further inland. Another wartime casualty was the oyster watchman's house, built in 1819 on the tiny island that you'll see just across the water as the harbour wall turns north. The house, which belonged to Matthew Russell, has never been rebuilt – but Russell's Lake still runs south from the island he once called home.

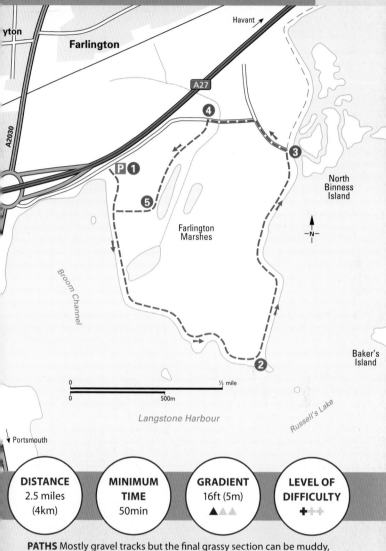

DISTANCE	MINIMUM TIME	GRADIENT	LEVEL OF DIFFICULTY
2.5 miles (4km)	50min	16ft (5m) ▲▲▲	✚✚✚

PATHS Mostly gravel tracks but the final grassy section can be muddy, particularly in winter **LANDSCAPE** Grazing marsh, wetlands and harbour wall **SUGGESTED MAP** OS Explorer 119 Meon Valley, Portsmouth, Gosport & Fareham **START/FINISH** Grid reference: SU 680044 **DOG FRIENDLINESS** On lead at all times **PARKING** Coastal car park by A27 (may be very busy at weekends) **PUBLIC TOILETS** None on route **NOTE** The harbour wall is very exposed and it can be surprisingly cold at any time of year, so do check the forecast and bring some warm clothing with you.

Opposite: HMS Warrior moored at Portsmouth

WALK 8 DIRECTIONS

❶ Leave the car park through the kissing gate beside the Wildlife Trust's notice boards and follow the gravel path down the slope. Walk through the bushes to a second kissing gate and zig-zag right, then left, up onto the harbour wall. The winding coastal path offers exceptional views across Langstone Harbour and turns hard left after almost 1 mile (1.6km).

❷ The scenery changes as you head north, with views to the Victorian forts along the top of Portsdown Hill. Continue past a viewing area and information panel, followed by an old wartime bunker, then keep an eye out for the low bulk of North Binness Island drawing closer on your right.

> **⚓ ON THE WALK**
>
> You'll get outstanding views across Portsmouth and the Isle of Wight on the early stages of your walk. Taller than Big Ben or the Blackpool Tower, the distinctive 558-feet (170m) Spinnaker Tower stands guard over the waterfont at Gunwharf Quays. The viewing decks include a chance to walk on Europe's largest glass floor.

❸ Turn left to pass between the two wooden field gates that cross your path and drop down off the harbour wall onto an enclosed track leading into the reserve. After 275yds (251m) turn left at the junction and pass the Wildlife Trust's whitewashed store building.

> **⚲ IN THE AREA**
>
> Eight hundred years of naval history awaits you at Portsmouth Historic Dockyard. Visit Nelson's iconic HMS *Victory* and HMS *Warrior*, the world's first iron-hulled warship, in an authentic setting of period naval buildings. Other attractions include the *Mary Rose* museum, harbour tours and the hands-on Action Stations experience. Site tickets are valid for a full year.

Continue walking to reach a kissing gate some 100yds (91m) further on.

❹ Turn left through the gate and follow the waymarked grassy path into the heart of the reserve, with reedbeds and an open wetland area on your left. Cross the small footbridge and continue for 200yds (183m), passing bushes and a couple of small ponds.

❺ Turn right across the grass to reach the kissing gate that you passed on your outward route. Turn right again and retrace your steps to the car park.

> **🍴 EATING AND DRINKING**
>
> Just 1.5 miles (2.4km) down Eastern Road on Portsea Island, the Great Salterns Harvester offers unlimited salad with its range of grills, burgers and family favourites. Turn the corner into Burrfields Road for sandwiches, baguettes and jacket potatoes, as well as pub classics and big plate specials at the Farmhouse Hungry Horse.

A SOUTH DOWNS VILLAGE HISTORY

Step back in time as you explore
the secrets of this East Hampshire village.

Lying at the foot of the South Downs, East Meon is a compact little community that began life in the shelter of Park Hill some 1,500 years ago. Later it became part of a royal manor belonging to Alfred the Great and by the time of The Domesday Book the village supported six mills and enough land for 64 ploughs.

Wartime Vandalism

East Meon's striking All Saints church also dates from shortly after the Norman Conquest and its spire stands on a central Norman tower of similar style and date to the tower of Winchester Cathedral. Norman windows appear in the nave and south transept and both the north and south doorways are of Norman origin. Another survivor from this time is the black Tournai marble font. One of only four in Hampshire, the font fell victim to Roundhead soldiers during the English Civil War; camping near East Meon before the Battle of Cheriton in 1644, the soldiers ripped out the font's lead lining to make their bullets. Four of the soldiers were later buried upright in the south transept, where their graves are marked by a carved stone with the words 'Amens plenty'.

More Architectural Curiosities

The church is just one of several interesting buildings that you'll pass on this walk, starting with Old Bell Cottage. Formerly the Bell Inn, the pub had its origins as the venue for a visiting cobbler who carried out shoe repairs while their owners sat drinking in an adjoining room. The building is now rented out as a holiday cottage.

Continuing past the recreation ground, you'll come to the 14th-century Court House. For centuries this was the administrative centre for the Bishops of Winchester and home to several monks who looked after the Bishops on their visits to East Meon. Once the scene of episcopal courts, by the early 20th century the building was being used to accommodate farm workers who kept their cows in the great medieval hall! The building was restored in 1927.

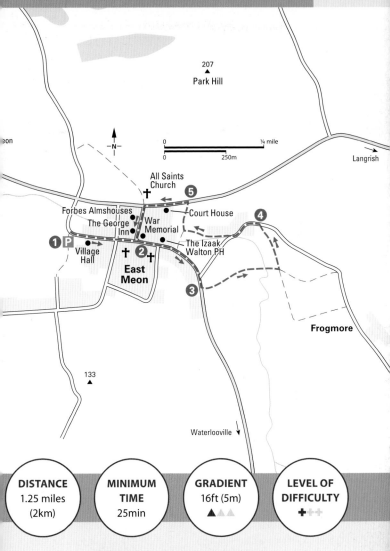

207
▲
Park Hill

—N—

0   ¼ mile
0   250m

→
Langrish

All Saints
Church
✝
5

Forbes Almshouses   ● ─ Court House
The George   ● War   **4**
Inn   ●   Memorial
1 P   ●   ─ The Izaak
Village   ✝ **2** ✝   Walton PH
Hall
**East
Meon**
3

Frogmore

133
▲

Waterlooville ↓

DISTANCE	MINIMUM TIME	GRADIENT	LEVEL OF DIFFICULTY
1.25 miles (2km)	25min	16ft (5m) ▲△△	✚✚✚

PATHS Village lanes and paths, 2 stiles
LANDSCAPE South Downs village setting
SUGGESTED MAP OS Explorer 119 Meon Valley, Portsmouth, Gosport & Fareham
START/FINISH Grid reference: SU 677222
DOG FRIENDLINESS Lead required through village lanes
PARKING Village car park, Workhouse Lane
PUBLIC TOILETS None on route

Opposite: East Meon

WALK 9 DIRECTIONS

❶ Walk back out of the car park and turn right along Workhouse Lane. Pass the village hall and the police house and keep ahead past East Meon Stores and the war memorial.

❷ Continue past Old Bell Cottage and the Izaak Walton pub across the stream to your left. Follow the road around to the right as far as the turning on your left towards Frogmore.

❸ Turn left here, then immediately right onto the signposted footpath across the recreation ground, with views of the brooding Park Hill on your left. Go through the gate on the far side of the recreation ground and follow the enclosed path to a stile. Nip across, turn left and continue through two gates and over a stile to a lane.

❹ Turn left; then, after 50yds (46m) fork right along the narrow path, keeping the stream on your left. Keep ahead at the footbridge and follow

the path to a kissing gate at a 3-way signpost. Turn right through the gate and walk beside the flint wall on your left to a kissing gate and road.

⊘ IN THE AREA

There's plenty to do in nearby Petersfield. Hire a boat on the 22-acre (9ha) Heath Pond, look round the 17th-century style Physic Garden or visit the town's museum to explore the area's social, industrial and agricultural history (open Tuesday to Saturday, March to December). The linked Flora Twort Gallery showcases the work of Petersfield's eponymous artist and Royal Academician.

❺ Turn left along the road and continue past the Court House, as far as the church. Turn left and walk down Church Street past the Forbes Almshouses, the village well and the George Inn. Turn right at Barnards Corner, keep ahead at the crossroads and retrace your steps to the car park.

🍴 EATING AND DRINKING

Choose from two pubs in the village centre. First comes the Izaak Walton, a friendly village local offering real ales, sandwiches, baguettes and home-cooked pub favourites, as well as a garden with children's play area. Towards the end of the walk you'll find winter log fires, a patio-style garden and a rather more formal menu at the George Inn.

🐾 ON THE WALK

Don't miss East Meon's colourful Millennium Embroidery in the north transept of All Saints Church. The 11ft (3.3m) panel, which depicts 107 houses, as well as birds, animals and local features, is displayed in a specially made cabinet with fibre optic lighting. Thirty people began work on the embroidery in 2000, finally completing their task in 2008.

EXPLORING ROMAN CALLEVA

Revealing the history of this once extensive
Roman town and its impressive surviving walls.

Tucked away in the gently undulating countryside between Basingstoke and Reading lies one of Hampshire's great enigmas. For here, among the web of narrow lanes that permeates the landscape of ancient woods and open farmland, you'll find the lost Roman town of Calleva Atrebatum.

An Abandoned Town

The Romans founded towns and cities across England from Dover to Exeter and Carlisle – but Calleva was different. For unlike most Roman centres, which have survived and developed into modern times, Calleva was simply abandoned. As a result you can still see most of the original Roman walls and the remains of the mighty gateways, which today stand guard over the quiet Hampshire countryside.

The lack of later development has given archaeologists a unique opportunity to excavate the interior and discover some of the secrets of this remarkable time capsule. Calleva was already the prosperous tribal capital of the Atrebates tribe and the administrative centre for a large area before the Romans developed the site after the invasion of AD43. It became a key military and commercial centre, with major roads radiating out to important centres including London, Winchester and Salisbury. Earth ramparts were built to protect the buildings in the late 2nd century and the facing walls that you see today were added between AD250 and 275. The wall is about 1.5 miles (2.4km) round and enclosed broad streets laid out on a grid pattern, with great public buildings and villas.

Digging Up History

The site was thoroughly excavated during Victorian times, exposing a partial plan of the road network, foundations of buildings and what is thought to be the earliest known Christian church in Britain. More recent excavations have revealed that Calleva was probably occupied until the 6th or 7th century – rather later than earlier evidence seemed to suggest. The buildings were later re-buried to protect them from the weather, vegetation and souvenir hunters.

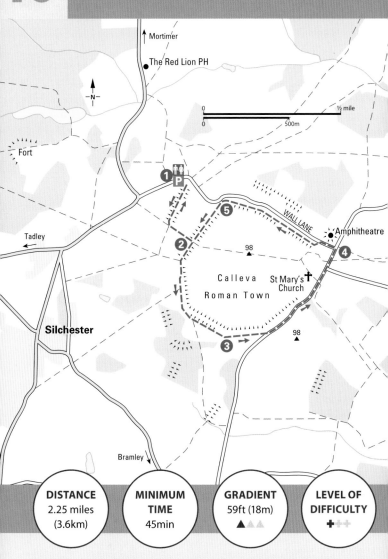

DISTANCE	MINIMUM TIME	GRADIENT	LEVEL OF DIFFICULTY
2.25 miles (3.6km)	45min	59ft (18m) ▲▲▲	✚✚✚

PATHS Grassy paths with short sections of woodland and road walking, 1 stile

LANDSCAPE Open farmland and mixed woodland

SUGGESTED MAP OS Explorer 159 Reading, Wokingham & Pangbourne

START/FINISH Grid reference: SU 635628

DOG FRIENDLINESS Keep on a lead near sheep

PARKING English Heritage car park

PUBLIC TOILETS Portaloo at the start

WALK 10 DIRECTIONS

❶ Leave the car park on the footpath just behind the flint information columns and follow it around the bend to a small wooden gate. Turn right, then bear left to reach the information panel at the end of the track that bisects the town.

❷ Turn right along the waymarked bridleway just inside the town wall and follow it for 100yds (91m) to a pair of kissing gates. Go through the right-hand gate and follow the tree-lined path on the outside of the wall. The wall here is little more than an overgrown bank with occasional patches of exposed masonry but beyond the trees it stands out clearly up to 15ft (4.6m) high.

🌿 ON THE WALK

A visit to the church of St Mary the Virgin, which dates from 1180 and features Roman bricks incorporated into the walls and buttresses, will reveal simple 13th-century wall paintings and an organ from about 1770.

🍴 EATING AND DRINKING

A short drive from the car park, the Red Lion in Mortimer West End is an attractive pub that dates back to 1575. You'll find a flower-filled front terrace, a beamed bar with low ceilings and log fires in winter, as well as real ales and an appetising menu.

---

❸ Pass the south gate and continue along the broad grassy sward until you reach a stile beside the gate leading out onto a lane. Turn left, still with the wall on your left and pass the car park by St Mary's Church. Keep ahead at the road junction and bear left at the letterbox into Wall Lane.

❹ Just here, a kissing gate on your right leads into the amphitheatre. Then continue along Wall Lane for 100yds (91m) and turn left through a wooden gate. Cross a plank bridge and continue through a kissing gate to climb the bank and turn right along the top of the Roman wall. Take care with children as the parapet is missing in places and there's a sheer drop on your right.

❺ The path descends at the north gate, then climbs again to follow the top of the wall. This section leads you back to the kissing gate where your circuit of the wall began (Point **❷**). Turn right beyond the gate and retrace your steps back to the car park.

🌍 IN THE AREA

Visit Reading Museum (closed Mondays) to see the Silchester Collection. The wealth of items from the Roman town includes coins, pottery, jewellery and inscribed tiles that help to interpret daily life during the Roman occupation. Most were found during excavations of the area between 1890 and 1909.

CRICKET ON THE DOWNS

Explore Hambledon, the village that nurtured
the English summer game more than two centuries ago.

While the origins of cricket may be lost in the mists of time, few places have
had such a hand in developing the game as the little village of Hambledon.
Tucked into a fold of the Downs on the edge of the Meon Valley, Hambledon's
cricket club dates from about 1750.

Following a Legend

By 1762, the legendary cricketer Richard Nyren had moved from Sussex to the
Hut, an isolated pub on Broadhalfpenny Down about 2 miles (3.2km) north-
east of Hambledon. The pub's name was soon changed to the Bat and Ball
and in 1764 Nyren led Hambledon to victory in a match against Chertsey.

For almost 30 years the men of Hambledon played their matches on
Broadhalfpenny Down, just across the road from Richard Nyren's pub,
which provided the players with ample hospitality and served as the club's
headquarters. On a notable occasion at Sevenoaks in 1777, the Hambledon
team defeated an England side in a match played for one thousand guineas
– and, by the close of the 18th century, the team had beaten their All England
opponents on several other occasions.

In 1772 Nyren moved into the centre of Hambledon to take over the much
larger George Inn. You'll see the former inn on the corner of East Street right
at the beginning of your walk, its signboard still projecting out over the road
from an impressive iron bracket. The club's headquarters moved with Nyren
and, within ten years, the club itself had transferred to its present ground at
Ridge Meadow on Windmill Down. Your route passes the ground, which was
also a more convenient base for enjoying Richard Nyren's lavish hospitality.

Throughout this period Hambledon was the centre of the cricketing
world. The club helped to develop the game with innovations such as length
bowling and the introduction of a third stump and it was widely accepted as
cricket's governing body. But the writing was on the wall as the century drew
to a close. In 1787 the Hambledon club's president, the Earl of Winchelsea,
was instrumental in founding the Marylebone Cricket Club, which rapidly
established itself as the leading authority on the English summer game.

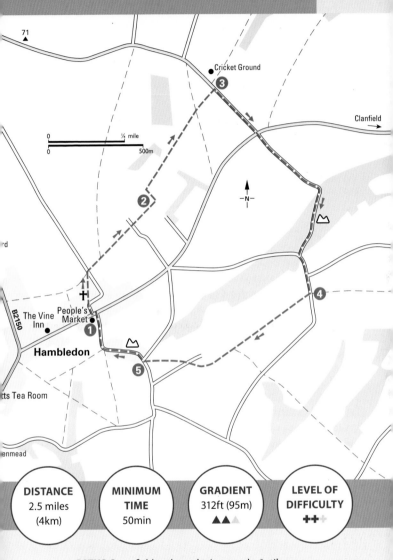

PATHS Cross-field paths and minor roads, 6 stiles
LANDSCAPE Rolling arable farmland with some woods
SUGGESTED MAP OS Explorer 119 Meon Valley, Portsmouth, Gosport & Fareham
START/FINISH Grid reference: SU 646150
DOG FRIENDLINESS Keep under close control and on lead near horses
PARKING Roadside parking in Hambledon village centre
PUBLIC TOILETS None on route

WALK 11 DIRECTIONS

❶ Walk up High Street and into the churchyard from the People's Market in the centre of the village. Fork right, cross the lane and follow the track beside the school, then continue along the enclosed footpath. Cross the private road and keep ahead through the vineyard to a stile.

❷ Nip across, turn left onto the track and continue up the narrow path to the left of the field gate for 60yds (55m) to a stile on your right. Cross over and walk towards the corner of the woods ahead. Cross the stile, zig-zag right and left, then follow the path diagonally across the open fields to a signpost and stile opposite Hambledon Cricket Club.

❸ Turn right down the lane, cross East Street and keep ahead towards Glidden Farm. Follow the lane as it climbs gently at first, then more steeply, to a junction; bear left and continue for 100yds (91m) until the road bends sharp left. Keep ahead for 80yds (73m) to a stile on your left.

❹ Turn right here, following the electricity wires across the open field to a stile. Continue through the

> ### ⌖ IN THE AREA
> Take in a fixture at one of the two village cricket grounds. Your route passes Hambledon Cricket Club's ground at Ridge Meadow on the outskirts of the village, while the Broadhalfpenny Brigands play opposite the Bat and Ball pub, about 2 miles (3.2km) up the road towards Clanfield. There are matches at both venues on most summer weekends.

narrow paddock, then swing right over the stile near the end of the paddock and cross the farm drive to continue along the narrow hedged path diagonally opposite.

❺ Turn half right down Speltham Hill and drop steeply back to the centre of the village where your walk began.

> ### 🌿 ON THE WALK
> Going up Hambledon High Street, you'll see a house on the left with a sign over the porch. This was the butcher's shop, run by William Langtry and his family from 1908 until after the Second World War. The shop is now a private house but you can still see the old meat hooks around the front of the building.

> ### 🍴 EATING AND DRINKING
> Brick floors, oak beams and a disused well await you at the friendly 16th-century Vine Inn. This proper village local serves real ales and Thatcher's ciders, as well as sandwiches, snacks and daily specials. Families and dogs are welcome. On the B2150, Lotts Tea Room opens early for breakfast and continues with hot meals and home-made cakes (closed Mondays).

A MEON VALLEY RIVALRY

Track the rise and fall of an ambitious
new railway that didn't deliver the goods.

More than half a century after the last public trains steamed along the Meon Valley Railway, your walk begins just off Station Road in West Meon's former goods yard. Now used as a car park for the popular 10-mile (16.1km) railway walk south to Wickham, there's still plenty to see here. The overgrown platforms stretch beneath the road bridge and if you've a head for heights you can walk out along the towering embankment to the start of the demolished viaduct.

A Railway Failure

The railway is an extraordinary tale of commercial rivalry and defeat snatched from the jaws of victory. By the end of the 19th century, the powerful London and South Western Railway was the dominant player in Hampshire and southern England. Its lines had already penetrated as far west as Padstow on the north Cornish coast – deep into the territory of its main competitor, the Great Western. For its part, the Great Western had driven south from Reading to Basingstoke and from Didcot to Winchester and now had the Portsmouth and south coast traffic firmly in its sights.

The London and South Western was having none of it. The company successfully promoted its own line south from Basingstoke, continuing down the Meon Valley to Fareham and effectively frustrating the Great Western's ambitions. The company spared no expense in laying out its new route with lavish stations, smooth curves and easy gradients designed to accommodate double track. Nevertheless, it started life in 1903 as a single track railway, with passing loops at the intermediate stations.

But it was to prove a hollow victory. With its heavy earthworks and tunnels, the Meon Valley line was expensive to maintain and the traffic in this thinly populated area simply didn't materialise. The railway was never upgraded to double track; services were progressively cut back and changes in the 1930s further downgraded the route's status and passenger appeal. The line couldn't compete in the harsh economic climate that followed the Second World War and all services were withdrawn in 1955.

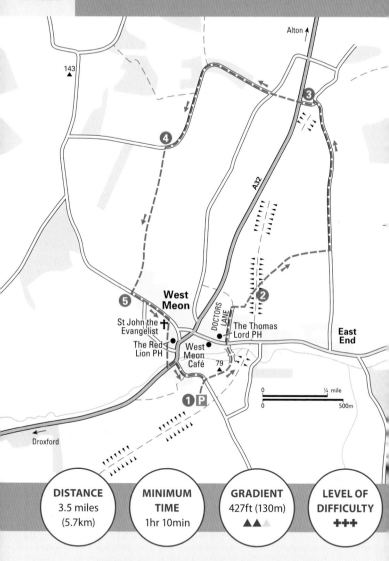

DISTANCE
3.5 miles
(5.7km)

MINIMUM TIME
1hr 10min

GRADIENT
427ft (130m)
▲▲▲

LEVEL OF DIFFICULTY
+++

PATHS Country tracks, minor roads and field paths

LANDSCAPE Rolling arable farmland with a few trees

SUGGESTED MAP OS Explorer 132 Winchester, New Alresford & East Meon

START/FINISH Grid reference: SU 642236

DOG FRIENDLINESS Keep under close control; lead required for crossing the A32

PARKING Meon Valley railway line car park

PUBLIC TOILETS None on route

WALK 12 DIRECTIONS

1 Walk back down the station approach, cross Station Road and take the signposted footpath opposite. Cross two footbridges, then turn left along the village road for 60yds (55m) before turning right up Doctors Lane. Walk between the gateposts at The Cedars, then fork right at the signpost, follow the path to a kissing gate and bear right to a second kissing gate.

2 Cross the old railway and walk diagonally across the field to a gap in the far left-hand corner. Bear right and cross the next field to reach a narrow lane. Turn left, continue over the hill and drop down across the old railway bridge to the A32.

3 Take great care as you cross the main road and keep ahead up the sunken track opposite. Cross a metalled lane, continue along the signposted bridleway and keep ahead past Highfield House. Now follow the track as it curves left, continue for 430yds

🐾 ON THE WALK
Turn right briefly when you reach the River Meon near the start of your walk to see the massive concrete foundations of the former railway viaduct. The engineers had originally planned a conventional arched crossing of the valley but the soft ground forced them to extend the embankments and erect a 62ft (19m) high steel viaduct instead.

(393m) and keep right at a junction until the track bears right again.

4 Turn left at a waymarked barrier in the hedge and follow the grassy track down through the shallow valley to reach the road at Hill View.

5 Turn left past Long Priors, keep ahead over the low summit and turn right into the churchyard. Turn left at the church porch, follow the path out of the churchyard gate and keep ahead to the A32. Cross over with care, zig-zag left and right into Station Road and continue up the station approach to the car park.

🍴 EATING AND DRINKING
West Meon Café opens daily for breakfast, light lunches, cakes and hot drinks (closed Sundays in winter) and you'll also find two pubs. The Red Lion a traditional village local that welcomes walkers and their dogs; expect real ales, pub grub and a relaxed summer garden. For a more formal menu, head for the Thomas Lord.

🕮 IN THE AREA
Take a look around West Meon's Church of St John the Evangelist. Sir George Gilbert Scott's pleasing Gothic Revival building was consecrated in 1846. Thomas Lord, the founder of Lord's Cricket Ground, is buried in the churchyard.

ADVENTURES IN THE CANDOVERS

This trail of amateur archaeologists and powerful bankers unravels the history of a Victorian church.

Walking up beside the cricket field towards the trim and neatly-kept Church of St Peter and its impressive row of yew trees, the words 'media frenzy' and 'Brown Candover' seem unlikely bedfellows. And yet, in 1928, correspondents from titles as diverse as *The Times* and the *Children's Newspaper* were converging on the Candover Valley. Television was still in the future but Brown Candover was featured on the radio and in local papers from as far away as Yorkshire and Chiswick.

Old William's Tale

The seeds of this story were sown in the 19th century, when the parish of Brown Candover had been merged with neighbouring Chilton Candover. The little church at Chilton Candover became redundant and was pulled down in 1876 – and over the years, the old churchyard became overgrown and neglected. When the rector, Revd Gough, decided to tidy it up, he struck up a conversation with 80-year-old William Spiers who had lived in the village all his life. Old William told the rector that he remembered kicking skulls around in 'a great old place' underneath the churchyard when he was a boy.

In the best traditions of Victorian amateur archaeology, Revd Gough called in his son and the two men started to dig. The press was quick to catch on. Was it an underground church? A Roman temple? Everyone seemed to have different ideas, though the structure was eventually identified as a Norman crypt with a barrel-vaulted nave and lancet windows. Inside the crypt was the 14th-century tomb of John of Candover.

A Victorian Replacement

The little building is on private land but you'll see its successor easily enough on this walk. Largely financed by the wealthy Baring banking family who lived at nearby Northington Grange, St Peter's church was built in 1844 to replace the dilapidated medieval building. It was designed by T H Wyatt, who later worked on new assize courts in Winchester and went on to become President of the Royal Institute of British Architects.

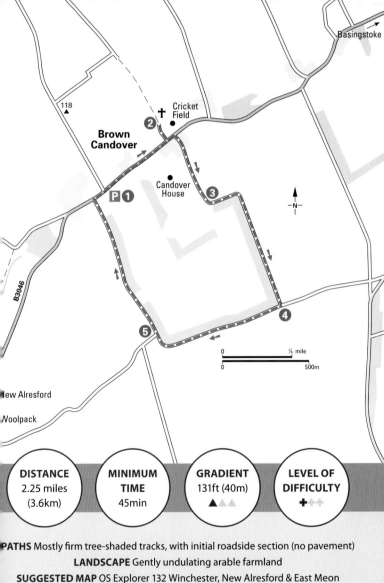

○ **DISTANCE**
2.25 miles
(3.6km)

○ **MINIMUM TIME**
45min

○ **GRADIENT**
131ft (40m)
▲▲▲

○ **LEVEL OF DIFFICULTY**
✦✦✦

PATHS Mostly firm tree-shaded tracks, with initial roadside section (no pavement)

LANDSCAPE Gently undulating arable farmland

SUGGESTED MAP OS Explorer 132 Winchester, New Alresford & East Meon

START/FINISH Grid reference: SU 578393

DOG FRIENDLINESS Keep on lead (shooting country)

PARKING Large roadside lay-by on B3046, centre of Brown Candover

PUBLIC TOILETS None on route

WALK 13 DIRECTIONS

1 Turn right out of the lay-by and walk north-east along the B3046, leaving the Woodmancott turning behind you. Turn left onto the Wayfarer's Walk after about 0.25 miles (400m) and walk up the side of the cricket field to visit the church.

2 Return to the road and zig-zag left and right onto the restricted byway. Pass Barn Cottage and continue along the firm track, with glimpses of the impressive 18th-century Candover House through the hedge on your right.

🐾 ON THE WALK
Mounted on the west wall of St Peter's church, just inside the main door, you'll find a monumental brass that dates back to the reign of Henry VIII. The brass, which came from the old church and was placed here in 1889, is unusual because the two figures are standing arm in arm.

3 Turn left at the top corner of the field, keeping the line of trees on your right, then follow the track as it swings to the right and continue up the gentle slope to a T-junction.

4 Turn right onto the waymarked off-road cycle trail that runs along the Ox Drove. The track follows a gentle switchback, then bends sharply right to reach a junction by some large modern barns.

5 Keep ahead past the barns onto a surfaced farm lane and continue down the hill to the B3046. Turn right at the bottom for the short distance back to your car.

🍴 EATING AND DRINKING
Local produce features strongly at the stylish Woolpack Inn in Totford, just down the road towards Alresford. Walkers, families and dogs are all welcome and there's a nice garden with children's play area for warmer days. Palmers Dorset ales support the blackboard and dining room menus, which include bar snacks, pub classics and à la carte options, as well as traditional roasts on Sundays.

🌢 IN THE AREA
Visit Northington Grange for an idea of the family that built St Peter's Church. The building that you'll see was converted from an earlier house with the addition of classical Greek façades shortly before the Barings bought it in 1817. Alexander Baring was created Lord Ashburton in 1835 and the family continued to adapt the house throughout the 19th century. The house was sold before the Second World War and suffered years of neglect after its last owner died in 1964. English Heritage has made many improvements since taking over the property in 1975 and today the building hosts an annual opera festival.

WILLIAM AND THE SILENT WHISTLES

A rural ramble around the royal hunting
ground of the Forest of Bere.

With its medieval market square and engaging collection of independent
shops, Wickham is one of Hampshire's most attractive little towns. It was the
birthplace of William of Wykeham, founder of both Winchester College and
New College, Oxford.

From Humble Beginnings

Despite his humble peasant background William led a charmed life and by
the time he was appointed Bishop of Winchester in 1367 he was a wealthy
man. He transformed the interior of his Norman cathedral and personally
endowed the two prestigious colleges that still flourish more than 600 years
after his death. William had been educated in Winchester, where he caught
the eye of Bishop Edington, who introduced him to Edward III.

In a secular career spanning 20 years, William rose to be Chief Surveyor
of the Royal Castles and Warden of Forests and Woods. It was a fitting
appointment, for in those days Wickham lay at the heart of the Forest of Bere,
a vast woodland stretching from the Sussex border to the River Test. Saxon
kings hunted here since long before the Norman Conquest but in 1086 King
William formally declared Bere as a royal hunting forest. When Charles I
led the last royal hunt in 1628, most of the trees had been felled to provide
timber for the naval dockyards along the south coast.

Railway Comings and Goings

Nevertheless, timber remains an important industry and a large timber yard
still flourishes beside the former railway goods yard at Mislingford. The Meon
Valley railway arrived late on the Hampshire landscape, a product of territorial
skirmishing between rival railway companies (see Walk 12). From the start
it generated little revenue and drifted through the inter-war years towards
the inevitable closure in 1955. Yet the railway has its place in history. Early in
June 1944, Sir Winston Churchill and his War Cabinet met other Allied leaders
in a special train at Droxford Station to complete their plans for the D-Day
invasion of Europe.

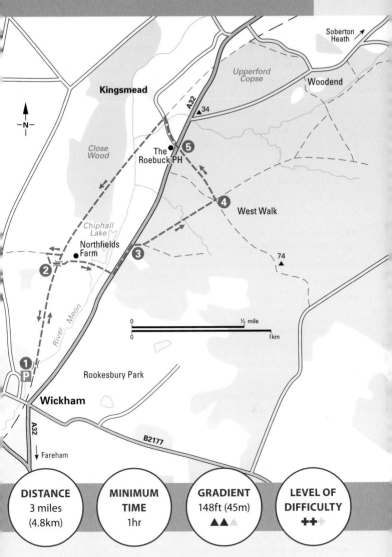

DISTANCE
3 miles
(4.8km)

MINIMUM
TIME
1hr

GRADIENT
148ft (45m)
▲▲▲

LEVEL OF
DIFFICULTY
+++

PATHS Bridleways and forest tracks (may be muddy)
LANDSCAPE Old railway path, river valley and mature woodland
SUGGESTED MAP OS Explorer 119 Meon Valley & Portsmouth
START/FINISH Grid reference: SU 574116
DOG FRIENDLINESS Can run free on the old railway and in West Walk
PARKING Station car park, Wickham
PUBLIC TOILETS Station Road, Wickham

WALK 14 DIRECTIONS

❶ The station car park on the north-east outskirts of Wickham backs directly on to the bridleway. Turn left, heading north and leaving the bridge over the River Meon behind you. Follow the old line as far as the first overbridge; then, 60yds (55m) beyond the brick arch, take the path that doubles back to the left and climb up to the farm track at the top.

❷ Turn left, cross over the railway and follow the track as it winds past Northfields Farm and Chiphall Lake to the A32. There's no footway here so cross over, turn left and take great care as you follow the busy main road for 200yds (183m), passing two lodge cottages on the right-hand side.

❸ Just beyond Chiphall Paddock, turn right past a barrier into West Walk. Follow the track at right angles to the road for 75yds (69m), then fork left onto a forest path. Ignore all turnings and keep ahead as the trail dips into

> ### 🦋 ON THE WALK
> The lavish scale of the bridges and earthworks along the old railway path tell their own tale of thwarted ambition. Although the line was built wide enough for double track, it opened with just a single line – and traffic was so disappointing that the second track was never laid.

a valley, crosses a brook and climbs 300yds (274m) to a five-way junction.

❹ Take the second exit left and continue for 60yds (55m) to a Pilgrims Trail marker post on your left. Fork left here, follow the narrow woodland path gently downhill and keep ahead at waymarked crossways to a plank bridge. Turn right and continue to the A32 opposite the Roebuck pub.

❺ Cross this busy road with care and continue down Kingsmead. Just before the old railway bridge turn right down the slope onto the old line, then turn left under the bridge for the final 1.25 miles (2km) back to the start.

> ### 🍽 EATING AND DRINKING
> Wickham offers a good choice of pubs, restaurants and tea rooms at the beginning or end of your walk. Half-way round, pop into the Roebuck for lunchtime sandwiches, ploughman's and jacket potatoes amid the bookshelves and a unique collection of show-biz memorabilia. There's also a full menu of cooked dishes, with a traditional roast on Sundays.

> ### 🏛 IN THE AREA
> Children will love the secret tunnels and underground chambers at Fort Nelson. One of a chain of Victorian forts on Portsdown Hill, it was built to defend Portsmouth from the threat of a Napoleonic invasion that never came. The fort is open daily (except Christmas).

A WATERCRESS WALK

Exploring the 'new market' town at the
heart of Hampshire's watercress industry.

New Alresford (pronounced Allsford) is not very new at all. In fact, this
delightful place, one of Hampshire's most picturesque small towns, was 'new'
in 1200, when Godfrey de Lucy, Bishop of Winchester, wanted to expand the
original Alresford – Old Alresford.

Georgian Architecture

Most of the medieval timber-framed houses were destroyed by two fires
during the 17th century, one in 1644 when the Royalists set the town alight
following the Battle of Cheriton. As a result, much of the architecture is
Georgian, notably along sumptuous Broad Street which is lined with limes
and elegant colour-washed houses. Mary Russell Mitford, the authoress of
Our Village which sketches her country life, was born in Broad Street in 1787.

Close to both Old and New Alresford you will find an intricate network of
crystal clear chalk streams, rivulets and channels that form the rivers Arle
and Itchen and the Candover Stream. Since Victorian times these springs
and rivers have played a vital role in one of Alresford's major industries, the
production of watercress. Surprisingly, watercress never stops growing in
the spring water that emanates from the ground at a constant 51 degrees
Fahrenheit throughout the year. These ideal growing conditions made
Alresford the 'Watercress Capital' of England, with the railway providing the
vital link by transporting watercress to London and much of the country.
The watercress beds continue to thrive in this health-conscious age.

You'll pass several watercress beds where you can see how the water is
collected in concrete channels and pumped back up again. You'll also pass
the 300-year-old, thatched and timber-framed Fulling Mill which straddles
the River Arle. Here, home-spun wool was scoured, washed, pounded with
mallets, stretched, dried, brushed and sheared. Old Alresford is tiny, with an
interesting 18th-century church and two substantial Georgian houses. Make
time to visit the church to see the monument to Jane Rodney. Admiral Lord
Rodney, who is buried in the family vault, built Old Alresford House and is
famous for defeating the Spanish fleet off Cape St Vincent in 1780.

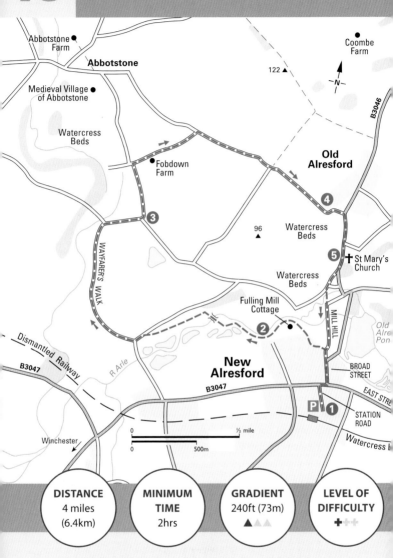

WALK 15 DIRECTIONS

❶ From the car park walk down Station Road to the T-junction with West Street. Turn right, then left down Broad Street and keep left at the bottom along Mill Hill. Half-way down turn left into Ladywell Lane and soon join the river bank and pass the attractive, timbered and thatched Fulling Mill Cottage which straddles the River Arle.

🍴 EATING AND DRINKING

The Globe in New Alresford offers good pub food, decent ale and wine and views across Alresford Pond from its waterside garden. Alternatively, try the Horse and Groom or, for good light lunches and teas, Tiffins Tea Room, at the bottom of West Street.

---

❷ Continue to the bottom of Dean Lane and keep to the riverside path. Cross a footbridge over the river and ascend to pass some cottages. Shortly afterwards, a lane merges from your right; follow it for 50yds (46m), then fork right onto the Wayfarer's Walk and continue to a junction of tracks. Bear right uphill to a lane.

❸ Turn left, descend to Fobdown Farm and take the track on the right beside the farm buildings. At a T-junction of tracks, turn right and follow the track for just over 0.5 miles (800m), gently descending into Old Alresford.

❹ Pass watercress beds on your right and follow the now metalled lane left, past houses. Turn right beside the green to reach the B3046. Cross over and follow the pavement right to a lane opposite St Mary's Church.

❺ Having visited the church, cross the road and turn left along the pavement to a grass triangle by a junction. Bear right along the lane and take the footpath ahead over a stream and beside watercress beds back to Mill Hill and Broad Street.

🐾 ON THE WALK

Enjoy a steam train ride on the Watercress Line between New Alresford and Alton. It was from here that watercress was transported to London and there are four stations, sheds and special events.

🔎 IN THE AREA

Note the Old Sun, a former pub, in East Street, where John Arlott, the cricket commentator and writer, lived. In the churchyard you'll find the graves of French prisoners of war, who died in the village while on parole during the Napoleonic Wars. More unusually, the grave of a stray dog called Hambone Junior can be found close to the River Arle. It was adopted by American soldiers waiting at Alresford for the D-Day invasion in June 1944 but was run over and killed.

Fulling Mill on the River Arle, New Alresford

TALKING RABBITS AT ECCHINSWELL

Explore the scenery that inspired Richard Adams' best-selling novel *Watership Down*.

The rolling chalk hills around Ecchinswell leapt to fame in 1972 as the backdrop for Richard Adams' first novel *Watership Down*. The book later became the best-selling Penguin novel of all time and was the inspiration for Art Garfunkel's British number one hit 'Bright Eyes', commissioned for the 1978 film version of the story.

Rabbits' Tales

Adams' narrative traces the fortunes of a small band of rabbits who set out into the unknown after one of their number, the clairvoyant Fiver, foresees the destruction of their warren at Sandleford. Leaving many of their fellows behind, the group unites under the gentle leadership of Fiver's brother Hazel and embarks on an epic journey to find a new home.

After setting up home near the north-east corner of the beech hanger on the lofty heights of Watership Down, Hazel realises that his new warren of buck rabbits has no future without female company. Helped by Kehaar the seagull, the rabbits locate an overcrowded warren at Efrafa and the second half of Adams' book recounts their epic struggle to liberate some of the does from the warren's tyrannical ruler General Woundwort.

Meanwhile, Hazel leads a daring raid on nearby Nuthanger Farm, where an earlier sortie had discovered four rabbits – two bucks and two does – living in captivity. The caged rabbits are eventually rescued from their hutch and return to the warren at Watership Down; but, in the confusion, Hazel suffers a gunshot wound that will trouble him for the rest of his life.

In the early stages of the walk you'll meander beside a tiny brook before striking out across farmland that would be familiar to the heroes of Adams' novel. Then, you'll climb beside woodlands for open views over the valley towards Watership Down and the narrow beech hanger where the rabbits established their warren. This is the countryside that Hazel's raiding party crossed on their way to the next landmark on your walk, Nuthanger Farm. Beneath its tall brick chimneys and clay tile roof, this charming building can have changed little since Adams first described it some 40 years ago.

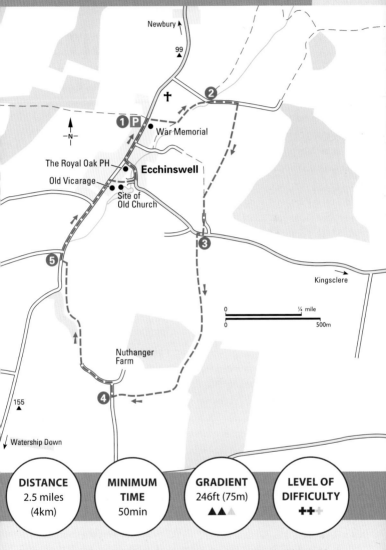

DISTANCE
2.5 miles
(4km)

MINIMUM TIME
50min

GRADIENT
246ft (75m)
▲▲△

LEVEL OF DIFFICULTY
✚✚✚

PATHS Country tracks, field and woodland paths (may be muddy), 2 stiles
LANDSCAPE Wooded farmland with downland views
SUGGESTED MAP OS Explorer 144 Basingstoke, Alton & Whitchurch
START/FINISH Grid reference: SU 500597
DOG FRIENDLINESS On lead near grazing livestock and the woods before
Nuthanger Farm **PARKING** Village hall car park, opposite the war memorial
PUBLIC TOILETS Swan Street, Kingsclere

WALK 16 DIRECTIONS

❶ Leave the car park by the vehicle entrance, cross the road and take the footpath beside the war memorial. After a few paces bear left onto a narrow woodland path, cross a plank bridge and continue past a turning on your right to the T-junction by a waterworks building.

❷ Turn right, cross the stream and continue for 150yds (137m) before turning off onto the waymarked path across the open field on your right. Continue through a gap in the opposite hedge, then follow the winding hedge on your right to the stile in the far corner of the field. Nip over and cross the next field to reach the road at a gate.

❸ Turn left along the road for 60yds (55m) and turn right onto the signposted footpath. Keep ahead along the top of a wooded bank, climb to the corner of the copse on your right and continue along the enclosed path beside the copse. Bear right as the path matures into the grassy farm track leading to Nuthanger Farm.

> ⓘ **EATING AND DRINKING**
>
> Local ales and home-cooked meals await you in the cosy bar of the Royal Oak, which also offers a newly refurbished restaurant. Behind the pub, the riverside garden is the venue for summer barbecues, as well as al fresco cocktails served from the thatched rumshack. Dogs are welcome on their leads.

❹ Turn right at the T-junction, swing left at the farm gate and follow the winding drive to a wooden stable building. Dodge right here onto the narrow path that continues as a sunken way with open views towards Ecchinswell on your right. The path widens as it drops into the valley to meet the village lane by a red-brick cottage.

> ⓘ **IN THE AREA**
>
> Just a couple of miles to the west, Sandham Memorial Chapel is surely one of the National Trust's most unusual properties (open Wednesday to Sunday summer, weekends only rest of year). The interior of this modest red-brick building is covered with dramatic paintings by Stanley Spencer (1891–1959), a medical orderly and soldier during the First World War. You're welcome to picnic amongst the fruit trees in the garden.

❺ Bear right along the lane, passing the small graveyard on your right. Just beyond the adjacent Old Vicarage, turn right along the path through the grassy site of the old church of St Lawrence. Cross the white-railed footbridge and turn left along the road to the junction by the Royal Oak; turn right here and walk past the school to the car park.

ROCKS AND ROYALS AT SARISBURY

Explore the extensive landscaped gardens
and grounds of Holly Hill.

With its links to royalty and the nobility, a stroll around Holly Hill Woodland Park is a cut above your average walk.

At the dawn of the Victorian age William Cawte owned much of Holly Hill but the landscape that you'll see on this walk was largely created for Quentin Hogg during the 1880s. An old Etonian who made his fortune in the tea and sugar trade, Hogg was a keen sportsman and social reformer. He was also the grandfather of another Quentin Hogg – the late Lord Hailsham, who served as Lord Chancellor in both the Heath and Thatcher governments.

It's rumoured that Hogg employed Sir Joseph Paxton, architect of London's Crystal Palace, to design his gardens. What's more certain is that the grottoes and waterfalls at Holly Hill were constructed by James Pulham and Son, a prominent firm of landscape gardeners who also worked for the royal family at Sandringham and Buckingham Palace. Although the Pulhams used natural stone for their gardens wherever possible, their 'rock builders' also developed the technique of creating artificial Pulhamite rocks like the ones you'll see at Holly Hill. These rocks were built up around a brick or rubble core and faced with a mixture of cement and Portland stone, so that the finished job was almost indistinguishable from the real thing. The company went out of business in about 1940 but not before leaving other examples of their work in major gardens throughout Britain.

Winn's Developments

After Quentin Hogg's death in 1903 the estate was sold to George Winn, who built the mansion and laid out the sunken garden a few years later. You can see the sunken garden near the picnic area, just after crossing the old carriageway at the start of your walk and you'll also get glimpses of the private mansion from here. Further on, as you walk around the lakes, you'll see examples of the ornamental specimen trees planted since the late 19th century. One of the oldest is a Californian coastal redwood, a species that's always popular with children who can punch its soft, thick bark without hurting themselves. Just make sure that they find the right tree.

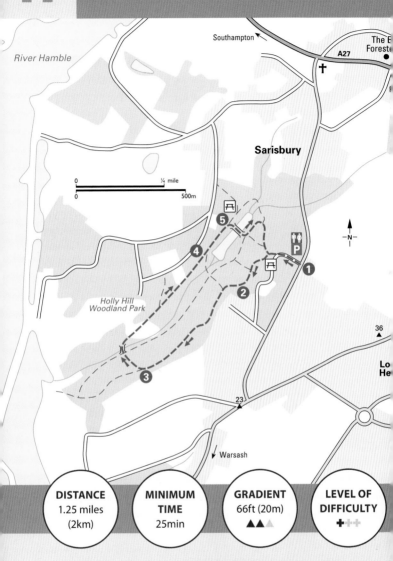

DISTANCE	MINIMUM TIME	GRADIENT	LEVEL OF DIFFICULTY
1.25 miles (2km)	25min	66ft (20m) ▲▲▲	✚✚✚

PATHS Firm woodland paths **LANDSCAPE** Landscaped wooded valley, lakes and waterfalls, with a flight of 21 steps

SUGGESTED MAP OS Explorer 119 Meon Valley, Portsmouth, Gosport & Fareham

START/FINISH Grid reference: SU 501078

DOG FRIENDLINESS Keep under close control

PARKING Holly Hill Woodland Park car park, Barnes Lane

PUBLIC TOILETS At the start

WALK 17 DIRECTIONS

1 Leave the car park by the gate and keep ahead along the woodland path to a junction with the old carriageway. Turn left, pass the picnic area on your left and turn right at the next junction.

2 Follow the path to a marker post and fork left. Keep ahead past a gateway on your left, ignore the turning on your right and continue to a small clearing and bench seat.

3 Fork right here onto a narrow path, turn right at the T-junction and keep ahead across the footbridge at the foot of a short slope. Pass a pair of water pipes that bridge the brook on your left, keep ahead along the boardwalk

> ### 🌿 ON THE WALK
> Holly Hill is a designated nature conservation site with flourishing flora and fauna. In summer you might spot holly blue or purple hairstreak butterflies in the wooded areas and attractive yellow flag irises fringe many of the lakes.

and continue through this quiet valley beside the brook to the Cawtes Copse information panel on your right.

4 Keep ahead for 100yds (91m), then turn left at the lake, cross the stepping stones and turn right. Walk past the old carved tree trunk and follow the path as it winds uphill past the Pulhamite grotto and runs parallel with the edge of the lakes to a picnic area.

5 Turn right across the waterfall bridge, then left across the smaller footbridge and continue beside the lakes on your left. A few paces after crossing a second bridge over a small stream turn right, cross another bridge and keep ahead up the woodland path. Follow it as it swings sharp right, then turn immediately left up a flight of steps to the gateway into the car park.

> ### 🍴 EATING AND DRINKING
> Colourful hanging baskets and a large garden give the Bold Forester at Sarisbury Green an inviting look from the outside. Inside, you'll find scrubbed wooden tables, real ales and a menu that works its way from hot jacket potatoes right through to steaks and fresh fish. There's a children's adventure playground and summer barbecues, too.

> ### 🏞 IN THE AREA
> Manor Farm Country Park features a working Victorian farm set in 400 acres (162ha) of scenic countryside beside the River Hamble but conveniently located just a few minutes from the M27 (junction 8). Farm animals roam free in the authentic farmyard and there's also a wheelwright's shop, forge and Victorian schoolroom. Refreshments are available from the Pantry Tea Room.

SALT, SAND AND SOLENT

From woodland to waterside, this varied
route offers a breath of sea air.

From its enviable position at the mouth of the River Hamble, Warsash
commands far-reaching views across Southampton Water and the Solent
to the Isle of Wight.

Salty Traditions at Newtown

Modern Warsash has extended south to encompass the former hamlet of
Newtown, right at the mouth of the Hook River. Here, the Warsash Maritime
Academy upholds a local tradition that dates back more than six centuries.
You'll see its Southampton University campus as you turn inland from the
beach, close to the site of a naval dockyard that provided 11 ships and more
than 200 men at the time of the Hundred Years War with France.

When the French wars ended in the mid-15th century, Newtown turned
its energies to farming, fishing and smuggling, as well as to the production
of sea salt. For hundreds of years this was a profitable business along the
Hampshire coast – but, in the face of competition from the Cheshire salt
mines and punitive taxation to fund the Napoleonic Wars, the industry simply
collapsed. By the middle of the 19th century, a chemical works had sprung up
in the place of Newtown's salterns; an iron works soon followed and in 1865
Newtown Road was built to connect the new industries with Warsash.

The new road prompted more development and, meanwhile, William
Hornby had bought the neighbouring estate at Hook and built a large
country house. A later member of his family, Arthur Hornby, persuaded the
Ecclesiastical Commissioners that a new church was needed to serve the
area's growing population. He gave the land and endowed St Mary's church,
which you'll see at the very start of your walk. It was consecrated in 1871.

In modern times, the River Hamble is a major sailing centre. Warsash
supports a sailing club and the Royal Yachting Association's headquarters
are across the water at Hamble-le-Rice. Every summer the yachtsmen get out
of their boats for one of the most eccentric fixtures of the sporting calendar.
As the Brambles sandbank rises in mid-Solent on the lowest tide of the year,
sailing club crews race out there for an annual cricket match on the sands.

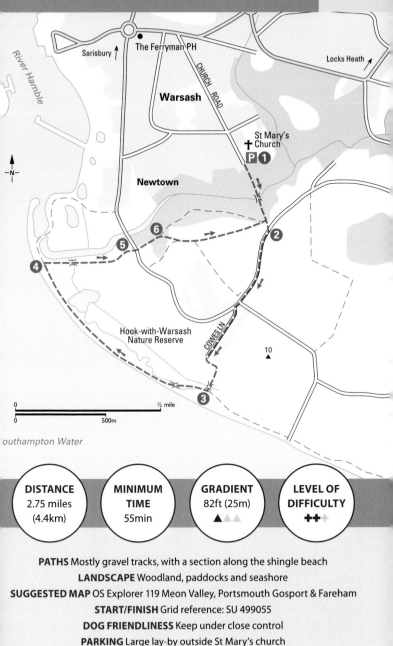

DISTANCE	MINIMUM TIME	GRADIENT	LEVEL OF DIFFICULTY
2.75 miles (4.4km)	55min	82ft (25m) ▲▲▲	++✦

PATHS Mostly gravel tracks, with a section along the shingle beach

LANDSCAPE Woodland, paddocks and seashore

SUGGESTED MAP OS Explorer 119 Meon Valley, Portsmouth Gosport & Fareham

START/FINISH Grid reference: SU 499055

DOG FRIENDLINESS Keep under close control

PARKING Large lay-by outside St Mary's church

PUBLIC TOILETS Warsash, beside the Ferryman pub

Warsash

WALK 18 DIRECTIONS

❶ Continue down Church Road with St Mary's on your left and keep ahead onto the waymarked off-road cycle trail. The trail drops gently, shaded by trees and rhododendrons, then crosses a stream and climbs to a crossways. Keep ahead for 50yds (46m) to a T-junction.

❷ Turn right onto the rutted gravel track, pass a couple of houses on your left and continue onto a residential road. A few paces further on, turn left into Cowes Lane. Follow this pleasant tree-lined road, keep ahead onto a gravelled private road and continue along the waymarked footpath that bends left at the entrance to Hook-with-Warsash Nature Reserve. Go through a kissing gate and bend right, then cross a footbridge to reach the coastal path at a second kissing gate.

❸ Turn right and walk along the beach for about 0.75 miles (1.2km) until the mouth of the River Hamble opens out

🍴 EATING AND DRINKING

Walkers and families are welcome at the Ferryman in the centre of Warsash. An interesting range of ciders complements real ales at the bar and the extensive menu includes sandwiches, jacket potatoes and burgers. There's also a good choice of salads, steaks, main course dishes and seafood.

and you reach the large lake at the mouth of the Hook River on your right.

❹ Double back to the right at the remains of two old concrete buildings, onto the narrow gravel path between the bushes. The path winds briefly around drainage channels, then heads inland in the shade of young oak trees, dogrose and buckthorn.

❺ Keep ahead through the gate at Christmas House, cross a road and continue along the signposted track opposite. Go through the kissing gate into Hook-with-Warsash Nature Reserve and continue for 130yds (119m) to a waymark post.

❻ Turn right, then left and follow the faint path across the grassy meadow with woodland on each side. Bear gently right, continue beside the wire fence at the far side of the meadow and into the trees to the kissing-gate at the crossways you passed earlier (Point **❷**). Turn left through the gate and retrace your steps to the church.

🚶 IN THE AREA

Take a trip on the little Hamble ferry, that runs regularly from its distinctive pink shelter on Warsash waterfront and you'll step ashore in Hamble-le-Rice just a few minutes later. The winding main street climbs the hill from the quay, making this popular sailing centre an attractive place to explore, or simply relax in one of several pubs and cafés.

ALFRED'S ANCIENT CAPITAL

Winchester's historic streets, Cathedral Close
and the beautiful Itchen Valley.

Historic Winchester, ancient capital of Wessex and England, was first settled in
the Iron Age and influenced by royalty since the 7th century. The city boasts
some remarkable architectural treasures.

Beginning from the imposing bronze statue of King Alfred the Great,
who made the city his capital, you have the choice of two walks. This walk
incorporates some of the famous sights, with a stroll through the water-
meadows to the Hospital of St Cross and St Catherine's Hill.

Winchester's Historic Streets

From the Victorian Guildhall, you walk up the High Street, which has been
a main thoroughfare to a crossing point on the River Itchen for some 2,500
years, before reaching the Cathedral Close. The cathedral was founded in
1079 on the site of an earlier building and remodelled in the 14th century. It is
the longest medieval church in Europe and among its treasures are the 12th-
century illuminated Winchester Bible, medieval paintings and the tombs of
early English kings and more recent notables, Jane Austen and Izaak Walton.

In the close you will find half-timbered Cheyney Court, formerly the
Bishop's court house. Beyond Kingsgate you'll pass the entrance to
Winchester College, founded in 1382 by William of Wykeham, the oldest
school in England. Join one of the guided tours (in summer only) to view the
handsome courtyards and cloisters, the chapel with its early 16th-century
stained-glass window and to savour the unspoiled medieval atmosphere. At
the end of College Street you'll see the Bishops of Winchester's house, the
surviving wing of a grand palace built in 1684 overlooking the striking ruins
of the 12th-century Wolvesey Palace.

Set in the wide, lush water-meadows beside the Itchen, at the end of the
beautiful riverside walk beside the College grounds, is the Hospital of St Cross.
Founded in 1132, it still functions as an almshouse and is the oldest charitable
institution in the country. Here you can visit the fine Norman church, the
Brethrens Hall and medieval kitchen and take the 'Wayfarer's Dole' – bread
and ale – a tradition that survives from the Middle Ages.

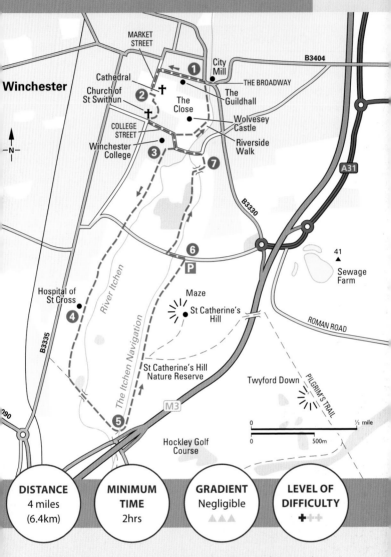

Winchester

MARKET STREET

B3404

① City Mill

Cathedral

② Church of St Swithun

THE BROADWAY

The Guildhall

The Close

Wolvesey Castle

COLLEGE STREET

Winchester College

③

Riverside Walk

⑦

-N-

A31

B3330

⑥ Ⓟ

Hospital of St Cross

④

River Itchen

41 ▲

Sewage Farm

Maze
St Catherine's Hill

ROMAN ROAD

The Itchen Navigation

St Catherine's Hill Nature Reserve

Twyford Down

PILGRIM'S TRAIL

M3

⑤

Hockley Golf Course

0   ½ mile
0   500m

DISTANCE	MINIMUM TIME	GRADIENT	LEVEL OF DIFFICULTY
4 miles (6.4km)	2hrs	Negligible ▲▲▲	✚▸▸

PATHS Established riverside paths through water-meadows, 3 stiles
LANDSCAPE City streets, riverside, water-meadow and downland
SUGGESTED MAP OS Explorer 132 Winchester
START/FINISH Grid reference: SU 485294
DOG FRIENDLINESS Under control through water-meadows and by golf course
PARKING Pay-and-display car parks in city centre
PUBLIC TOILETS The Broadway, Winchester

Opposite: Winchester Cathedral

WALK 19 DIRECTIONS

❶ From King Alfred's statue on the Broadway, walk towards the city centre, passing the Guildhall (tourist information centre) on your left. Join the High Street, then in 100yds (91m), turn left along Market Street. Continue ahead on to Cathedral Green to pass the cathedral's main door.

❷ Turn left down a cloister (signed to Wolvesey Castle), then right through the Close to Cheyney Court and exit via Prior's Gate. Turn left though Kingsgate, with the tiny Church of St Swithun above, then turn left down College Street and shortly pass the entrance to Winchester College. Beyond the road barrier, turn right along College Walk, then turn right at the end of the wall, along a college access road.

🍴 EATING AND DRINKING

Old pubs, tea rooms and restaurants abound around the cathedral and its close. Try the excellent Cathedral Refectory or the Courtyard Café behind the Guildhall, or the Wykeham Arms, in Kingsgate Street.

❸ Go left by a private entrance to the college. Follow the path beside the River Itchen for 0.5 miles (800m) to a gate and road bridge. Cross over and follow the riverside gravel path to a gate and cross open meadow towards the Hospital of St Cross.

🕑 IN THE AREA

Allow time to visit Winchester's City Museum on the edge of the Cathedral Green. It tells the story of the city, as an important Roman town and the principal city of King Alfred, through Anglo-Saxon and Norman England to modern times.

❹ Keep left alongside the wall and through an avenue of trees to a stile. Keep ahead on the path to two further stiles and join a farm track leading to a traffic-free lane. Turn left and continue across the River Itchen to reach a junction of metalled paths by the M3.

❺ Turn left along a path. Go under an old railway and pass a gate on your right (access to St Catherine's Hill). Keep left at a fork and drop down to follow a path by the Itchen Navigation. Go through the car park to the road.

❻ Turn left across the bridge and take the footpath right. Keep to the path beside the water, disregarding the path left (College nature reserve). Soon cross the bridge by rowing sheds to join a metalled track.

❼ Turn left, then left again at the road. Follow it right along College Walk and turn right at the end to pass the Old Bishops Palace (Wolvesey Castle) and follow the riverside path to Bridge Street, opposite the City Mill. Turn left to King Alfred's statue.

WILLIAM COBBETT'S 'UPHUSBAND'

See the village loved by the classic author and influential political activist.

The political campaigner William Cobbett wrote chapters of his classic *Rural Rides* in the early years of the 19th century, while staying with his friend Joseph Blount at Rookery House on Hurstbourne Hill. In his book he referred to the village many times by its contemporary name of Uphusband.

Crime and Punishment

The two men had much in common and both had served prison sentences for their radical views. In spite of this, the two friends continued to champion the rights of ordinary working people.

Blount was known for serving pork and potatoes to poor travellers from a wayfarers' table set up in front of his house and would lend his horse Tinker to help wagons up the long slopes of Hurstbourne Hill. Meanwhile, Cobbett began promoting his radical views in his newspaper, the *Political Register*.

After an interlude in the US, Cobbett returned to England in the aftermath of the Peterloo Massacre of 1819. He spoke out against the use of armed force to break up the political demonstration and stood, unsuccessfully, for Parliament in the following year. Cobbett then embarked on the project for which he is, perhaps, best remembered today, riding though south-east England and the Midlands to see the hardships endured by the rural poor.

Cobbett serialised his experiences in his own *Political Register*, before publishing the two volumes of *Rural Rides* in 1830. Nevertheless, he still aspired to a Parliamentary seat as the most effective way to improve the lives of ordinary people. After further electoral defeats, he was finally returned as MP for Oldham after the landmark Reform Act of 1832. At Westminster Cobbett spent much of his time as an advocate of the Poor Law, which was passed just a year before he died in 1835.

A short diversion from the centre of the village will take you to Blount's home at Rookery House. It's not open to the public – but right at the start of your walk you can seek out his grave in St Peter's churchyard. Then, as you descend from Doles Wood on the slopes of Hurstbourne Hill, you'll see the view that William Cobbett believed was one of the finest in southern England.

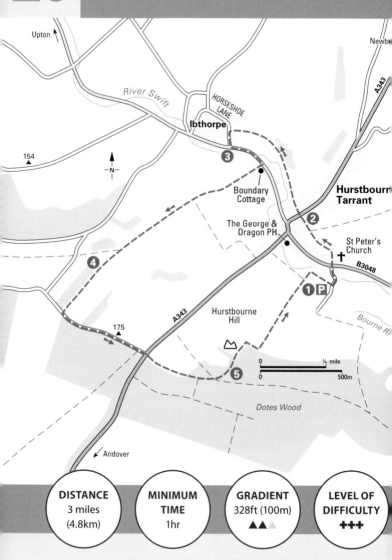

DISTANCE
3 miles
(4.8km)

MINIMUM TIME
1hr

GRADIENT
328ft (100m)
▲▲△

LEVEL OF DIFFICULTY
+++

PATHS Field and woodland paths (some overgrown or muddy sections), 3 stiles
LANDSCAPE Farmed valley with woodland on the upper slopes
SUGGESTED MAP OS Explorer 131 Romsey, Andover & Test Valley
START/FINISH Grid reference: SU 385528
DOG FRIENDLINESS Lead required through paddocks near the start
PARKING Parish car park, up the lane opposite the church
PUBLIC TOILETS None on route

WALK 20 DIRECTIONS

❶ Walk back to the B3048 and turn left past the school for 100yds (91m). Cross over, turn right through the kissing gate and bear left up the slope through a grassy paddock. Bear left through the kissing gate near the top and follow the enclosed path to the A343 near the village shop.

❷ Cross the road and follow the path beside Marine Cottage, going through a series of gates as you cross the paddocks, to join the fenced path towards a large thatched barn. Just before the barn, turn left through the gate and follow the track to meet Horseshoe Lane, turning left to the village road.

🍴 EATING AND DRINKING

Standing prominently in the heart of Hurstbourne Tarrant, the George and Dragon is a friendly village drinkers' pub with a beamed interior and sheltered patio garden. Local real ale and sandwiches are on offer, as well as morning coffee but don't expect cooked meals. Closed on Mondays.

❸ Cross and turn left. Pass the former Methodist chapel and turn right up the track immediately before Boundary Cottage. Climb steadily to the stile that marks a fork in the path. Keep ahead over the second (left-hand) stile and briefly follow the left-hand hedge before crossing the field towards the left-hand corner of the woods ahead.

⚓ IN THE AREA

Life-size models and dioramas feature alongside artefacts from Danebury hill-fort (see Walk 24) at Andover's Museum of the Iron Age. Together with material from other local sites, the museum tells the story of Hampshire life in the Iron Age and Roman periods. There's also a gift shop and light refreshments.

❹ Nip over the stile and follow the path to a lane, then turn left to reach a junction with the A343. Cross the main road and keep ahead along the edge of Doles Wood, ignoring the track on your right just after the woods close in on your left. Then, 100yds (91m) further on, turn left at the waymark post and bear right along a woodland path that drops to the corner of a wire fence.

❺ Follow the waymarked route steeply downhill beside the fence to reach a field. Turn right for 100yds (91m) along the woodland edge, then turn left and drop down towards the village. At the foot of the hill go through the gate into the recreation ground and turn right to the car park.

🐾 ON THE WALK

As you approach the church from the lychgate, you'll see Joseph Blount's grave on the left, at the foot of an ancient yew tree. Blount wanted his gravestone to be large and flat enough for children to play marbles on it. Families, please note!

THE ALLIES' GIANT LEPE

Explore one of Hampshire's most important wartime sites at Lepe Country Park.

More than two years of military planning went into the invasion of France on D-Day, 6th June, 1944. To move some 160,000 men across the English Channel on a single day would have been an extraordinary feat in peacetime. To have achieved it in wartime under heavy fire seems little short of miraculous, Yet, within three months, the Allies had over 2 million men in northern France. By the end of June, the Allies would need a cross-Channel harbour roughly the size of Dover to handle 12,000 tons of stores and 2,500 vehicles each and every day – so they took a couple with them.

Operation Mulberry and PLUTO

The Mulberry harbours were a civil engineering project of epic proportions. At least ten of the country's largest construction companies were called in to manufacture the many different components that were needed, including the massive 'Phoenix' caissons built here at Lepe. They were built at various locations around the British coast, launched on slipways like the ones you'll see on your walk, then towed to Selsey or Dungeness where they were stored on the seabed to avoid detection. When the invasion came, the caissons were re-floated and towed across the Channel to France.

Besides vehicles, stores and personnel, an advancing army needs fuel. Tankers were considered vulnerable to enemy attack, the vagaries of the weather and, in any case, were needed elsewhere. The military solution, developed in partnership with the Anglo-Iranian Oil Company, was PLUTO – the pipeline under the ocean.

In September 1944 these two pipelines began delivering 100,000 gallons (454,600 litres) of fuel a day to the Allied forces in France. Eventually a further 17 lines were laid from Dungeness and by VE Day in May 1945 the network had supplied more than 172 million gallons (167.5 million litres) of fuel.

You'll see plenty of reminders of Lepe's former wartime role as you walk along the beach. It's worth picking up one of the excellent leaflets from the information area beside the beach café before setting out, to help you interpret what you're looking at.

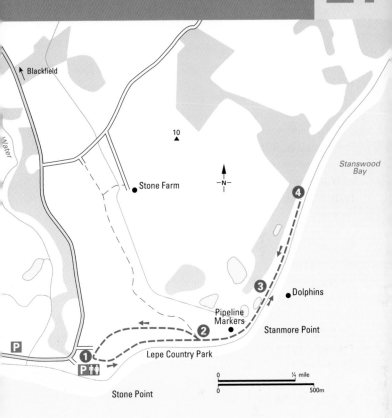

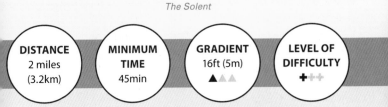

DISTANCE	MINIMUM TIME	GRADIENT	LEVEL OF DIFFICULTY
2 miles (3.2km)	45min	16ft (5m) ▲▲▲	✚✚✚

PATHS Sand and shingle beach, also gravel and grassy paths
LANDSCAPE Coastal scenery with adjoining meadowland
SUGGESTED MAP OS Explorer OL22 New Forest
START/FINISH Grid reference: SZ 455985
DOG FRIENDLINESS No dogs on the adjoining family beach (just off this route)
April–September **PARKING** Country Park car parks (pay-and-display)
PUBLIC TOILETS At the start

WALK 21 DIRECTIONS

1 From the beach car park, walk up the gravelled slope to the right of the café and then turn right along the gravelled path at the top of the low cliff. (From the upper car park, just head towards the cliff and then urn left). Pass the war memorial and continue between the gateposts to reach the wide sandy track behind the beach.

2 Pass the yellow gas pipeline markers at Stansore Point, where the track merges with the shingle bank and continue past the 'Dolphins'. These two historic offshore structures are all that remains of the former pierhead and mark the start of the D-Day construction area.

3 Walk to the end of the construction platforms. The seaward side is badly eroded at the northern end but you can still see the rolling track walls and get a good idea of the scale of this project.

4 Turn and retrace your steps to Point **2**. Rejoin the gravelled path as it bears inland past the gate on your right; then 60yds (55m) further on, turn right through the gap into the wildflower meadows. Follow the right-hand hedge until the faint grassy path swings left through the trees into the upper car park. Walk past the children's play area and down the slope to the beach car park.

🍴 EATING AND DRINKING

The smart, newly refurbished Beach Café is right at the start of this walk, offering hot and cold snacks and drinks.

🐾 ON THE WALK

There are two war memorials on your route. The first, beside the large anchor on the clifftop path, commemorates the 50th anniversary of D-Day in June 1994. Then, on the beach construction site, you'll see a plaque in memory of the Royal Dragoon Guards who sailed from Lepe to Gold Beach on 3rd June, 1944.

🌿 IN THE AREA

Visit the renowned 200-acre (81ha) Exbury Gardens, founded by Lionel de Rothschild in 1919 (open March to November). Still owned by the Rothschild family, the spectacular displays of rhododendrons, camellias and azaleas change colour with the seasons, making this a lovely place to visit at any time. A miniature steam railway runs through part of the garden.

TEST VALLEY OVERVIEW

Spectacular scenery, ancient earthworks and glorious wildlife characterise the downs overlooking Stockbridge.

The high slopes of Stockbridge Down command outstanding views of the Test Valley, which includes some of Hampshire's most alluring rural scenery. Picturesque villages with their ancient churches, pubs and thatched cottages lie folded into the chalk downland, linked by quiet lanes and rural paths.

From a walker's perspective, the 44-mile (71km) Test Way path starts close to the Berkshire border at Inkpen Beacon and follows the River Test until it flows into Southampton Water near Eling tide mill. The greater part of the route between Andover and Romsey runs over the former 'Sprat and Winkle' railway line, which closed in 1964. Though nominally independent, the railway sprang out of territorial battles between the London and South Western Railway and its arch-rival the Great Western. After Lord Palmerston cut the railway's first sod in 1859, much of the line was constructed over the former Redbridge Canal, so that today's walkers still follow a route that was first laid out in 1792.

Down to Business

This walk begins through scrub and light woodland on the lower slopes, dominated by species such as buckthorn, blackthorn, dogwood and juniper. Climbing towards the summit, the route passes the ramparts of the late Iron Age Woolbury hill-fort, thought to have been built in about 500BC. You'll see the impressive south-western ramparts, which are the only portion of the fort in National Trust ownership. There's little evidence that the interior of the fort was ever used intensively, though a small settlement on the eastern side was still occupied in Roman times.

Beyond the fort, you'll reach the more open downland and begin dropping down towards the main road. You may see grazing animals here, helping to keep the landscape clear of invasive scrub and you'll pass one of the 14 Bronze Age burial mounds scattered around the site. This is the place to look for typical chalk grassland wild flowers such as cowslips, harebells and horseshoe vetch, as well as characteristic butterflies including the brown argus and chalkhill blue.

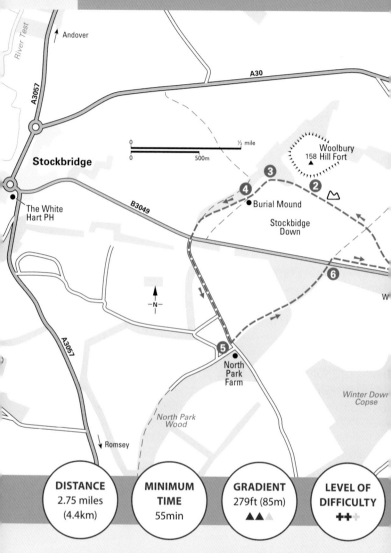

DISTANCE	MINIMUM TIME	GRADIENT	LEVEL OF DIFFICULTY
2.75 miles (4.4km)	55min	279ft (85m) ▲▲▲	++ +

PATHS Downland and field-edge paths, minor road and woodland tracks, 1 stile
LANDSCAPE Downland and wooded arable farmland
SUGGESTED MAP OS Explorer 131 Romsey, Andover & Test Valley
START/FINISH Grid reference: SU 387344
DOG FRIENDLINESS Keep on the lead near grazing animals and on roads
PARKING National Trust car park
PUBLIC TOILETS Stockbridge High Street, by Three Cups Inn

WALK 22 DIRECTIONS

❶ Leave the car park and follow the path ahead through woodland. Cross a footpath at a gate on your right and keep ahead up the valley as the woodland falls away on your left. Continue climbing through the trees and emerge at the clearing with the ramparts of Woolbury ahead.

❷ Carry on up the hill, bearing gently right as the path brushes the ramparts near the original southern entrance to the fort. Ignore the turning left and continue beside the ramparts for about 100yds (91m). Keep ahead as a second path leads off beside the ramparts and curve left through woodland beside the wire fence on your right.

❸ Keep straight on at the end of the trees across rising downland. Pass a bench seat on your left and keep ahead along the grassy path, passing between clumps of bushes and forking right to pass a fenced burial mound.

🍴 EATING AND DRINKING

You'll find plenty of choice in Stockbridge's attractive High Street, which has been voted 'Britain's best foodie street' by users of Google's Street View. Try the 15th-century White Hart for pub classics in a family atmosphere, or head for the stylish Thyme & Tides deli/bistro where the menu includes a selection of quiches, terrines and light bites as well as croissants, pastries and fresh fish specials.

🚶 ON THE WALK

Near the summit of the Down you'll pass a bench seat in memory of Professor Rosalind Hill. Her father, the prominent solicitor Sir Norman Hill, bought the Lordship of the Manor when he retired to Stockbridge in 1921 and the rights passed to his daughter soon after his death in 1944. A few years later, Professor Hill gave Stockbridge Down and the low-lying Common Marsh to the National Trust.

❹ Ignore the path that swings off left towards the car parks and keep ahead towards the bushes in the far right-hand corner of the site. Go through the gate, cross the B3049 with care and continue down the lane opposite. Continue for about 0.5 miles (800m) until you reach North Park Farm.

❺ Turn left onto the signposted footpath and follow the edge of the woods on your right. Dodge right and left at the corner of the field, cross the stile and follow the path beside woodland. Keep ahead past a broken stile at the corner of the field, continuing through the woods for 100yds (91m) back to the B3049.

❻ Cross with care and keep ahead through the pedestrian gate into the National Trust site. Turn right almost at once and follow the grassy track parallel with the road and into the trees. Finally swing left, then right, back to the car park.

FACTS AND FANCIES AT SHATTERFORD

Abundant wildlife and amazing legends
await you along this delightfully easy route.

This is a lovely, largely level route across the wide open heaths between Lyndhurst and Beaulieu, brushing the edges of ancient woodlands and passing a couple of ponds. And, while the route can be boggy in places, you'll cross most of these areas on well-engineered bridges and causeways.

The varied habitat means that this is a great place for wildlife. You're almost certain to see ponies, especially along the edges of the woodland, where you may also catch sight of fallow deer. The New Forest's wetlands are internationally important and these are the places to look for scarce plants like cottongrass, bog orchid and insectivorous sundews, with the possibility of seeing amphibians such as rare great crested newts in the ponds. Higher up, Dartford warbler, woodlark, common redstart and hobby have all been seen around Shatterford.

The Crawls

Along your way you'll cross the Bishop of Winchester's Purlieu, an area of some 500 acres (203ha) of heathland shaped like a distorted dumbbell and enclosed by the Bishop's Dyke – a low bank and ditch about 4.5 miles (7.2km) long. Now the dull truth is that no one seems very sure about the origins of this 3ft (0.9m) high earthwork. It's been suggested that it might have enclosed a large decoy pond, which is a plausible idea as the area is very damp and the bank largely follows a level course. Another idea is that the dyke formed the boundary of a medieval deer park, though the low banks and boggy nature of the ground makes this seem less likely.

But local tradition alleges that in the late 13th century Edward I offered to grant Bishop John de Pontoise as much land as he could crawl round in a day. Unlikely as this might seem, the tale is remarkably similar to that of Hampshire's 12th-century Tichborne Dole. In accordance with Lady Tichborne's dying wish, flour is still 'doled out' annually to the people of this Itchen valley village, after her miserly husband agreed to give her all the corn from an area she could crawl round whilst holding a lighted torch. Eight centuries later, the 23-acre (9.3ha) field is still known locally as the Crawls.

Opposite: Ponies grazing near Ipley

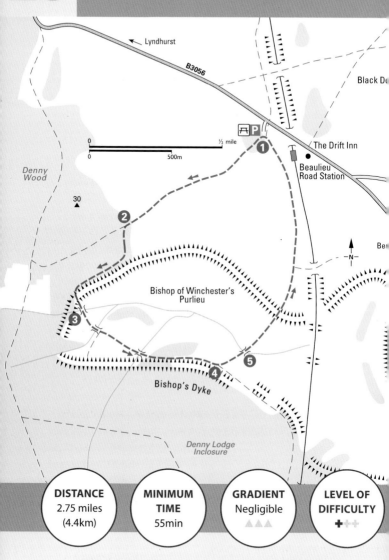

Lyndhurst

B3056

Black D[...]

The Drift Inn

Beaulieu
Road Station

Denny
Wood

30

Bishop of Winchester's
Purlieu

Be[...]

N

Bishop's Dyke

Denny Lodge
Inclosure

DISTANCE	MINIMUM TIME	GRADIENT	LEVEL OF DIFFICULTY
2.75 miles (4.4km)	55min	Negligible ▲▲▲	✚✚✚

PATHS Mostly firm heath and woodland paths (muddy in places)
LANDSCAPE Lowland heath and deciduous woodland edge
SUGGESTED MAP OS Explorer OL22 New Forest
START/FINISH Grid reference: SU 348063
DOG FRIENDLINESS Keep under control near grazing ponies
PARKING Shatterford car park
PUBLIC TOILETS None on route

WALK 23 DIRECTIONS

❶ With your back to the car park entrance, turn right at the Shatterford name board and follow the broad grassy swathe through the pine trees and out onto the heath. Cross the causeway and footbridge, then follow the firm path across the heath, keeping left at the grassy divide. Keep left again after a few paces, taking the narrower grassy path between the outlying clumps of birch trees and the woods on your right.

❷ Follow the path into the woods, bear left and then curve right with the path as it tracks the woodland edge. The path drops gradually downhill, levels out, then swings left through the low bank of the Bishop's Dyke to a wooden-railed footbridge 100yds (91m) ahead.

❸ Turn left over the bridge, cross the short causeway and bear left over the larger of the two bridges ahead. Follow the broad grassy swathe across the heath and bear gently left over another bridge as the path picks its way between outlying trees and the woods on your right. Breaking clear of the trees, the path continues beside the woods to a large crater on your right.

> ### 🌐 IN THE AREA
> The awesome National Motor Museum is just one of Beaulieu's attractions. Others include the ruins of Beaulieu Abbey and the Secret Army Exhibition.

❹ Turn left at the grassy crossways just beyond the crater as the path ahead plunges back into the woods. Walk between a few scattered trees, then cross the pools ahead on two substantial wooden bridges.

❺ Follow the firm sandy track as it draws closer to the railway on your right. Pass the turning to a railway bridge on your right, cross a causeway and footbridge and follow the path back to the car park.

> ### 🍴 EATING AND DRINKING
> With its flagstone floors and photos reflecting the annual 'drift' or pony round-up, the Drift Inn is a welcoming place for locals, walkers and families with dogs. Open fires, comfy sofas and secluded tables set the scene, with an appealing modern British menu catering for every appetite. Children have their own menu and two garden play areas for children.

> ### 🦋 ON THE WALK
> The boggy part of the heath to the north of Denny Lodge Inclosure is a great place to look for dragonflies. The rare southern damselfly is one of over two dozen species that breed in the New Forest, which is considered to be the most important area in Britain for these colourful insects.

WAR AND PEACE AT DANEBURY

A stroll around one of Hampshire's most fascinating prehistoric sites.

Danebury Down has been crowned by its hill-fort for some 2,500 years. It stands in a commanding position, with views across the Test Valley to neighbouring Woolbury (see Walk 22) nearly 4 miles (6.4km) to the east. This short walk offers an enjoyable introduction to the site but do allow extra time to explore the centre of the ring and its massive outer defences.

The Community at Danebury

Danebury is one of Europe's most carefully studied hill-forts. Archaeologists believe that a community of three or four hundred people lived here for some five centuries until the Roman invasion in AD43. Their excavations have revealed the remains of 73 circular dwellings, as well as 500 store buildings and several thousand deep storage pits. These were probably used for holding grain, though only a few of the pits would have been used at any one time. Pagan shrines and temples were also found on the high ground near the middle of the fort. Here, offerings and sacrifices would have been made by the priests, who were also the community's legislators, teachers and medicine men.

   The Danebury community sheltered their sheep and cattle in the hill-fort and modern aerial surveys have shown up the remains of their prehistoric field systems in the surrounding landscape. Their farmers would have traded leather goods, woollens and grain for necessities such as iron, copper and salt. But life wasn't always so peaceful and while Danebury's warriors had helmets, swords and horse-drawn chariots at their disposal, at times everyone would have helped to defend the site.

Defending the Hill-fort

Indeed, the defences are the most obvious legacy of this Iron Age community. As you enter the fort you'll see the complex earthworks designed to make the enemy vulnerable as he zig-zagged towards the fort's massive timber gates. A stockpile of 11,000 pebbles found near this spot indicates that men, women and children may all have used slings to pelt their attackers with stones.

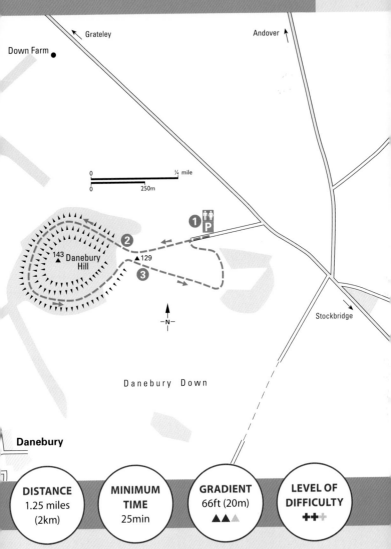

Grateley

Andover

Down Farm

0 — ¼ mile
0 — 250m

① 🚻 P

②

▲143 Danebury Hill

▲129

③

—N—

Stockbridge

Danebury Down

Danebury

DISTANCE	MINIMUM TIME	GRADIENT	LEVEL OF DIFFICULTY
1.25 miles (2km)	25min	66ft (20m) ▲▲▲	✦✦✦

PATHS Downland grass and gravel paths, two flights of steps
LANDSCAPE Wooded downs and grazing fields
SUGGESTED MAP OS Explorer 131 Romsey, Andover & Test Valley
START/FINISH Grid reference: SU 329377
DOG FRIENDLINESS No dogs inside the hill-fort gates; watch out for other colour-coded access areas **PARKING** Hampshire County Council car park
PUBLIC TOILETS At the start (open April–October) or Stockbridge High Street

WALK 24 DIRECTIONS

❶ Walk up the gravel path beside the toilet block and go through the wooden gate into the site. Follow the grassy path up the slope, aiming just to the right of the triangulation pillar on the outlying earthworks close to the fort entrance.

❷ Go through the gates at the entrance to the fort and follow the gravel path through the outer bank. Turn right, climb the 17 wooden steps up onto the inner ramparts. The ramparts were constructed by throwing back soil from the outer ditch behind a timber wall. In time the timbers rotted, creating the smoother profile that you'll see around the earth bank. Turn right along the top of the bank. From here, the circular gravel path leads right around the top of the defences. Drop down the 23 steps leading back to the main entrance. Turn right through the gates and bear right towards the triangulation pillar.

❸ Continue through the kissing gate straight ahead. Bear right, then left around the edge of this large field, where you may see grazing animals. Simply follow the field-edge around to the left until you reach the water trough and gate near the far corner. From here, follow the field-edge uphill for 100yds (91m) to a kissing gate and steps down into the car park.

⏱ IN THE AREA

Learn more about Danebury with a visit to Andover's Museum of the Iron Age (open Tuesday–Saturday), which brings the hill-fort to life with life-size models, reconstructions and dioramas. You'll also see some of the actual objects recovered from the site during Professor Barry Cunliffe's excavations.

🍴 EATING AND DRINKING

The Peat Spade Inn at Longstock offers real ales and a fine wine list, as well as an upmarket British menu based on fresh local produce to reflect the changing seasons. There are two sittings for the traditional Sunday roast and booking is strongly recommended. Alternatively, you'll find a good range of pubs and tea rooms in Stockbridge High Street.

🌿 ON THE WALK

Centuries of grazing have held back the scrub and native forest, creating the classic chalk grassland flora around Danebury. During the summer the characteristic wild flowers include common rock rose, wild thyme and salad burnet. Between May and August you'll see several species of orchid – the common spotted and pyramidal varieties are probably the easiest to identify.

MEANDERING AROUND MOTTISFONT

Combine glorious woodland and riverside walking, along the River Dun, with a visit to a 12th-century Augustinian priory.

This short walk explores the National Trust estate at Mottisfont. Set picturesquely beside the River Test and around the walls of a former 12th-century priory, Mottisfont is a charming village of thatched cottages and Georgian houses, complete with a splendid listed church and an old tithe barn. The village name is derived from 'moot's font' or 'spring of the meeting place', which rises in a deep pool in the abbey grounds.

Whether you start the walk from Mottisfont Abbey car park (seasonal opening) or from Spearywell Wood, you will find strolling through the village a real delight. Beginning from the latter, the walk explores good estate paths through woodland, then gradually descends into the Dun Valley, offering you serene views west across rolling downland into fertile Wiltshire.

The Abbey and St Andrew's

Originally an Augustinian priory church, founded by William Briwere in 1201, Mottisfont Abbey never achieved the full status of an abbey and struggled to survive until the Dissolution of the Monasteries. Between 1536 and 1540 it was acquired by William, Lord Sandys who converted the buildings into a mansion. It was during the 18th century that much of the medieval cloisters were destroyed and the romantic title 'abbey' given to the building. Although mainly private, you can still see some medieval arches, the 13th-century monks' cellarium and a masterpiece of trompe-l'oeil work by Rex Whistler, one of the great British artists of the 20th century, in the Drawing Room. You will find the sweeping lawns and mature trees which run down to the River Test very peaceful and well worth spending a few quiet moments in.

You should not miss St Andrew's Church in Mottisfont. Dating from the 12th century and Grade 1 listed, it contains more 15th-century stained glass that any other Hampshire church, a fine Norman chancel and a rare clock mechanism c1620, the only other one in working order is in Salisbury Cathedral. While strolling the magnificent grounds surrounding Mottisfont Abbey, look out for the old ice house behind the stables. Few remain in the county in such good condition.

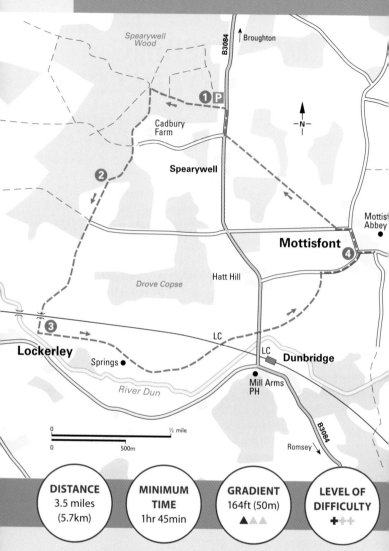

Spearywell Wood

Cadbury Farm

Spearywell

Mottisfont Abbey

Mottisfont

Hatt Hill

Drove Copse

LC

Lockerley

Springs ●

LC

Dunbridge

Mill Arms PH

River Dun

Romsey ↓

0 — ½ mile
0 — 500m

DISTANCE	MINIMUM TIME	GRADIENT	LEVEL OF DIFFICULTY
3.5 miles (5.7km)	1hr 45min	164ft (50m) ▲▲▲	✛✛✛

PATHS Easy woodland trails and field paths, 2 stiles
LANDSCAPE Water-meadows, farmland and National Trust woodland
SUGGESTED MAP OS Explorer 131 Romsey, Andover & Test Valley
START/FINISH Grid reference: SU 315277
DOG FRIENDLINESS Can be let off lead in Spearywell Wood
PARKING National Trust car park at Spearywell Wood
PUBLIC TOILETS In abbey gardens (only if visiting the Abbey)

WALK 25 DIRECTIONS

❶ Pass beside the barrier opposite the Spearywell Wood car park entrance to join a woodland path. Ignore paths left and right and pass through a tall conifer plantation; then, where the path reaches a junction, turn left (by a concrete marker stone). Bear right with the estate path at the next junction, then at the staggered junction (by a short cut sign to the abbey), bear left, then immediately right through woodland.

❷ Descend through the woodland fringe to a junction and turn left across a field. At a barrier and crossing of paths, zig-zag right, then left, following an estate path along the woodland edge. Continue beside fencing, eventually passing beneath the railway to a footbridge over the River Dun. The swiftly flowing River Dun, a tributary of the Test, was also known as the Barge River. At one time there were plans to develop a canal to link Southampton and Salisbury but the scheme was never completed.

❸ Don't cross the river. Turn left through the kissing gate and follow the path across meadow and marshy pasture, crossing two plank bridges to a double stile at the end by the oak trees. Bear right through a gate and follow the fence on your left. Continue through a copse, passing a spring, then an isolated thatched cottage to a stile by a gate. Proceed along the left-hand

field-edge and follow the grassy track to the railway. Cross the line (take great care – look and listen), then follow the track to a stile and the B3084. Turn right to visit the Mill Arms at Dunbridge. Cross to join a field path which soon bears left to a lane. Turn right and enter Mottisfont.

❹ At the T-junction, turn right for the entrance to visit Mottisfont Abbey. Retrace your steps along the road and bear right to a junction, opposite the abbey gates. Turn left along Bengers Lane and take the path right, diagonally across the field towards a lone oak tree. Cross a plank bridge and proceed through the next field to a gate. Turn right along the road for 150yds (137m) for the car park.

🍴 EATING AND DRINKING

The abbey has its own licensed restaurant. A short diversion just beyond half-way will lead you to the Mill Arms at Dunbridge for well-presented food, decent ales and a pleasant summer garden.

🌿 IN THE AREA

If you're here in June, make sure you see the National Collection of Old Fashioned Roses, in the walled kitchen garden of the abbey. The colour and heady perfume of thousands of roses on a balmy June evening is a magical experience.

PARK PALE'S KILLING FIELDS

Discover Lyndhurst's extraordinary
medieval earthworks and their royal pedigree.

Legend has it that Lyndhurst's Park Pale was originally built to round up the deer to make them easier targets for William II, whose aim is reputed to have been less than perfect.

The story has rather shaky foundations, since the Park Pale was first recorded in 1291 – and although this vast earthwork was by then already old, the date is almost two centuries after William's death in 1100 (see Walk 28). Whether or not King William was the inspiration for the work, its purpose is not in dispute. Building the Park Pale involved digging several miles of ditch and earth bank and this major construction project amply demonstrates the importance of venison in medieval times. After more than 700 years of erosion, about 3.4 miles (5.5km) of earthworks are still marked on modern maps and the original structure may have been significantly longer. Even today, the structure is as much as 29ft (8.8m) wide in places and the bank is up to 4ft (1.2m) high. When topped by the original wooden paling fence, Park Pale would have been a very effective barrier to even the most agile deer.

The existing structure has a wide, open entrance adjoining the present Park Ground Inclosure, with earthworks that curve around to a narrow closed neck not far from the start of your walk. Deer driven in from the entrance would soon have found themselves trapped and presented an easy target to the marksmen at the opposite end. You'll walk beside part of this section not long after setting out and cross it as you drop down to the Beaulieu Road.

Hotel with a History

After crossing the road, you'll follow a bridleway with views to the Parkhill Hotel. In the 13th century this was the site of a royal hunting lodge that was rebuilt by the Duke of Clarence in 1740. The building was modernised again a century later, when visitors included Queen Victoria and her family. Then, in 1880, Mr Willingham Rawnsley – a brother of Canon Rawnsley, one of the founders of the National Trust – established a boys' school here. Later the house became a hotel but was requisitioned for military use in the Second World War, when it played its part in the preparations for D-Day.

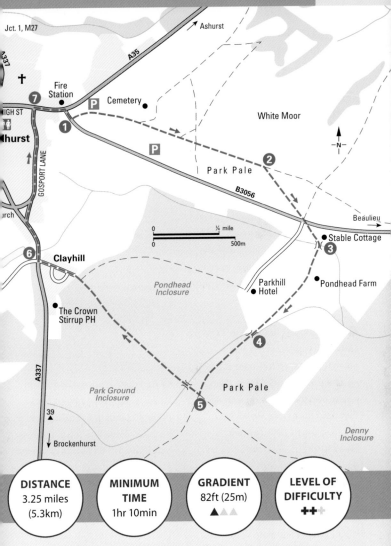

DISTANCE	MINIMUM TIME	GRADIENT	LEVEL OF DIFFICULTY
3.25 miles (5.3km)	1hr 10min	82ft (25m) ▲▲▲	+++

PATHS Heath and forest tracks, muddy woodland bridleway and roadside pavements **LANDSCAPE** New Forest heath and deciduous woodland **SUGGESTED MAP** OS Explorer OL22 New Forest
START/FINISH Grid reference: SU 303081
DOG FRIENDLINESS On lead along roads and near grazing animals
PARKING Bolton's Bench car park
PUBLIC TOILETS Lyndhurst, main car park

WALK 26 DIRECTIONS

1 Cross the car park access road, turn left and walk parallel with the road until it forks and swings left towards the cemetery. Rejoin the road here, then keep ahead along the track past a wooden barrier and continue across the heath for just over 0.5 miles (800m).

2 Fork right onto the wide grassy path, cross the low earthworks of Park Pale, then bear left as the path narrows and heads towards a junction on the B3056. Cross the road beside a small seasonal pond and take the left-hand fork towards Pondhead Farm.

3 Bear right past the drive to Stable Cottage, cross the white-railed bridge, then fork right at the entrance to Pondhead Farm. Keep ahead past the houses on your right, following the muddy woodland bridleway, with views towards Parkhill Hotel beyond the fence on your right. In the autumn months

you're quite likely to see pigs roaming in the woods beyond Parkhill Hotel.

4 Cross the footbridge and bear right, keeping within sight of the wire fence on your right, until you meet a gravelled track crossing your path.

⌖ IN THE AREA

Visit Alice Liddell's grave in Lyndhurst churchyard. Alice became the inspiration for *Alice in Wonderland* after meeting the Revd Charles Dodgson – alias Lewis Carroll – in Oxford, when she was just a little girl. In 1880 Alice married Reginald Hargreaves and moved to Cuffnells, near Lyndhurst. Following her death in 1934, her ashes were interred in the family grave.

---

5 Turn right, cross the bridge and follow this appealing forest track through stands of beech, oak and silver birch. Continue through a wooden gate, signposted towards Lyndhurst and keep ahead along the residential Beechen Lane to the A337.

6 Turn left here for a short diversion to the Crown Stirrup pub. Otherwise turn right along the roadside pavement and fork right along Gosport Lane, where the pavement continues on the other side, as far as the T-junction with Lyndhurst High Street.

7 Turn right, then right again opposite the Fire Station, to return to your car.

🍴 EATING AND DRINKING

The Crown Stirrup is a country pub on the outskirts of Lyndhurst serving real ales and home-cooked food. There's a garden with a play area, too. Alternatively, you'll find plenty of choice in Lyndhurst itself. Try the friendly Good Food Café for breakfast, lunch or an afternoon cream tea. Sunday roasts and children's options are also on the menu.

KEYHAVEN'S SOLENT SHORE

A stroll along the Solent Way and the wildlife-rich salt marshes south of Lymington.

Between Hurst Spit and Lymington lies the Lymington-Keyhaven Nature Reserve, a huge expanse of salt and freshwater lagoons, marshes and mudflats. This breezy, watery landscape with its distinctive plants and wildlife make these lagoons some of the most important in Britain. The area is a birder's paradise and the specialised wetland habitat attracts many rare and interesting species, particularly in the winter. From your vantage point on the sea wall you can scan the saltings and pools and see a wide range of waders and wildfowl. Guaranteed sightings will include heron, curlew, shelduck and skylarks. Walk this way in winter and you should see huge flocks of black-necked Brent geese feeding on the eelgrass, as well as long-tailed ducks, greenshanks and, out on the Solent, goldeneye and common scoter. The elegant common and sandwich terns, which breed on Hurst Spit, can be seen overhead during the summer and, if you're lucky, you may spot one of the rarer passage migrants, perhaps ruff, curlew sandpiper or little stint.

Extracting Salt

The area has not always been a refuge for wildlife, for salt production had been the principal local industry along this stretch of coastline since the time of *The Domesday Book* in 1086. At one time there were 13 saltworks on Keyhaven and Pennington marshes. Sea water was impounded in shallow tidal ponds, or 'salterns', each about 20ft (6m) square and left to evaporate. Once it had formed a strong brine, it was pumped by wind pump into boiling houses with coal-fired furnaces, where the water was boiled until salt crystals were left. Lymington salt was highly regarded and by the 18th century supplied much of southern England and was even exported to America. In 1800, 4,000 tons were produced, valued at one shilling (5p) a bushel (a bushel was equivalent to about 8 gallons/36.4L). It was already highly taxed but the cost of the Napoleonic Wars forced up tax rates to 15 shillings (75p) a bushel and when the new railways delivered cheaper rock salt from Cheshire the industry simply collapsed. Today, the old salterns that you can see from the sea wall are the best-preserved examples in southern England.

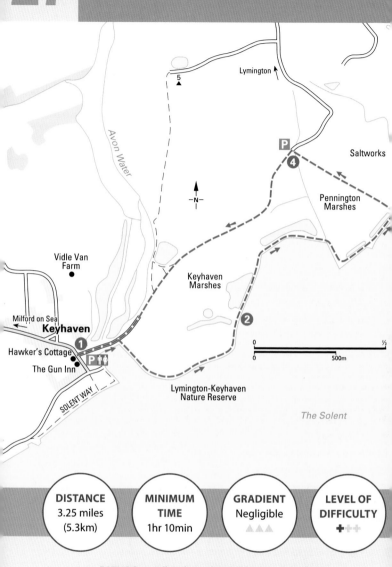

DISTANCE
3.25 miles
(5.3km)

MINIMUM TIME
1hr 10min

GRADIENT
Negligible

LEVEL OF DIFFICULTY

PATHS Sea wall path, tracks and short stretch of road
LANDSCAPE Salt and freshwater marshland
SUGGESTED MAP OS Explorer OL 22 New Forest
START/FINISH Grid reference: SZ 306914
DOG FRIENDLINESS Keep to the paths to avoid disturbing wildlife
PARKING Car park, Keyhaven (pay-and-display); limited free parking beside
the harbour wall **PUBLIC TOILETS** Keyhaven car park

WALK 27 DIRECTIONS

❶ Turn right out of the car park, then turn right again along the 'no through road' to follow the Solent Way along the harbour wall heading east. Turn right through the gate beyond the parking area and walk along the sea wall, with fine views across the Solent to Tennyson Down and Yarmouth on the Isle of Wight. Continue to a gate at the start of a long straight section.

❷ Follow the sea wall around the bay, with saltmarsh to your right and a large inland lagoon on the left keeping a sharp eye out for the reserve's rich birdlife. At length the sea wall turns sharp left and you'll come to a jetty with a red conical marker at the seaward end.

❸ Leave the sea wall here, turning left and heading down the slope on the track that cuts straight across Pennington Marshes to a small parking area on the far side of the Lymington-Keyhaven Nature Reserve.

❹ Turn left through the gate and onto the cycle path to Keyhaven, bypass another gate and then follow the well-made gravel track all the way back to Keyhaven. Keep ahead at the gate onto the metalled lane to the Solent Way gate and parking area that you passed earlier and retrace your steps to the car park.

> **🍴 EATING AND DRINKING**
> Right at the start of your walk, the Gun Inn has been licensed since at least 1886. Today it offers a garden and family room and the menu encompasses sandwiches, ploughman's and jacket potatoes, as well as a range of main course dishes and seafood. Hot drinks and home-made cakes are also available.

> **🦢 IN THE AREA**
> Take the ferry or walk along the pebble beach to Henry VIII's fortress at Hurst Castle. Completed in 1544 to defend the Solent's western entrance, Hurst was later used to imprison Charles I in 1648. The castle was strengthened in the 19th century and served as a coastal gun battery during the Second World War.

> **🐾 ON THE WALK**
> The imposing double-fronted Hawker's Cottage stands next door to the Gun Inn at Keyhaven. The house was built by the notable wildfowler Colonel Peter Hawker in 1818 and remodelled towards the end of the 19th century. After serving with the Duke of Wellington in the Peninsular War, Hawker kept a diary detailing 50 years of hunting on the marshes.

Hurst Castle and lighthouse

VIOLENT DEATH AT CANTERTON

Take a walk in the tranquil woodlands
with a troubled past on the edge of the New Forest.

Just across the road from the start of this walk, a triangular iron pillar marks
the spot where King William II, son of the Conqueror, met his death in August
1100. William, known as Rufus because of his ruddy complexion, was a
ruthless and unpopular king who showed little mercy to his subjects.

Regicide

The story of his death has been much embroidered in the telling over the
last 900 years and almost everything about it seems to be disputed. The
popular version is that William had spent the night before his death at a
nearby hunting lodge with some of his closest friends. There he had a vivid
nightmare, foretelling his death and though there are several different
versions of the dream, it seems to have affected William profoundly.

Nevertheless, the hunt went ahead. Before setting out, the King gave some
of his arrows to his friend Sir Walter Tyrrell, telling him that the best marksman
should have the best arrows – a prescient remark, as things turned out.
Towards sunset, Tyrrell and the king became separated from the rest of the
party. William fired an arrow at a passing stag, which was wounded but kept
running. Meanwhile Tyrrell let fly at another beast; but his arrow glanced off
the oak tree where the Rufus Stone now stands and hit the King in the chest.

William died instantly. Tyrrell fled to France and, according to some sources
had his horse's shoes reversed by a blacksmith so as to confuse any followers.
Perhaps he could have saved himself the expense, since a contemporary
source records that 'there were none to pursue him'. Indeed, fearing anarchy
after the King's death, the noblemen of the party abandoned his body and
galloped off to look after the interests of their own estates. Even William's
younger brother Henry made straight to Winchester to make sure of the
Treasury, before heading on to London to be crowned a few days later

It was left to Purkis, a local charcoal burner, to recover William's body and
take it on his cart to Winchester for burial beneath the tower of the Norman
cathedral. The King was little mourned and when the tower later collapsed on
his grave, it was widely believed to be a punishment for his wickedness.

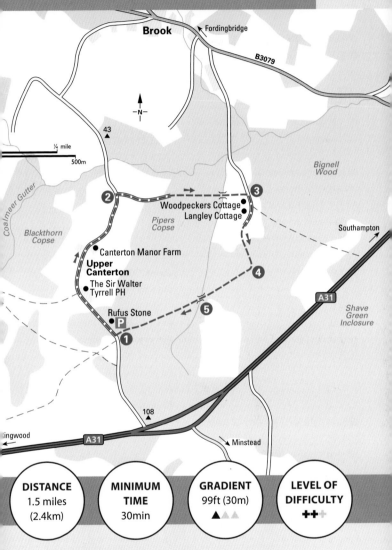

<table>
<tr><td>

DISTANCE
1.5 miles
(2.4km)

</td><td>

MINIMUM TIME
30min

</td><td>

GRADIENT
99ft (30m)
▲ ▲ ▲

</td><td>

LEVEL OF DIFFICULTY
✚✚✚

</td></tr>
</table>

PATHS Country lane, muddy tracks and woodland paths, ford

LANDSCAPE Deciduous woodland and forest clearings

SUGGESTED MAP OS Explorer OL22 New Forest

START/FINISH Grid reference: SU 270125

DOG FRIENDLINESS Lead required near grazing ponies

PARKING Rufus Stone car park

PUBLIC TOILETS None on route

WALK 28 DIRECTIONS

1 Turn right out of the car park and walk down the lane past the Sir Walter Tyrrell pub. Pass the picturesque Canterton Manor Farm and drop down the gentle slope to a letterbox by the road junction.

2 Turn right here between hedges of hawthorn, honeysuckle and dog rose and keep ahead onto the muddy bridleway at the end of the tarmac. Follow the track through the woods to a T-junction at Woodpeckers Cottage.

> ### ✿ ON THE WALK
> Five species of deer are found in the New Forest but you're most likely to see either fallow deer – which have distinctive creamy spots during the summer – or roe deer, with their characteristic black noses.

3 Turn right, pass Langley Cottage and, at the end of the track, bear left across the grass and through the trees to a clearing. Continue to the far right-hand corner of the clearing, about 250yds (229m) after leaving the track.

4 Turn right into the trees and follow the winding woodland path to the tiny ford near the corner of a fenced field on your left.

5 Jump the ford and then keep ahead up the slope through the beech, oak and holly trees to return to the car park.

> ### 🍴 EATING AND DRINKING
> Conveniently placed overlooking a New Forest lawn near the start of the walk, the Sir Walter Tyrrell also has a garden with children's play area. Expect Ringwood ales, Aspall's draught cider and a range of ploughman's, salads, pub classics and vegetarian fare; morning coffee and cream teas are also served daily. Dogs are welcome.

> ### 🌀 IN THE AREA
> Visit All Saints Church in nearby Minstead. With its chaotic layout, multiple levels and triple-decker pulpit, this extraordinary building is like something out of *Alice in Wonderland*. One of the three family 'pews' is in reality a small sitting room with padded seating and its own fireplace. Sir Arthur Conan Doyle and his wife are buried in the churchyard.

FLYING LOW AT STONEY CROSS

A classic New Forest pub is the highlight of this walk, exploring a wartime airfield.

No less than 12 specially constructed New Forest airfields played a key role in the Second World War, with sites that included Beaulieu Heath, Holmsley and Lymington as well as Hurn, which later became the civilian Bournemouth International Airport. Although the Forestry Commission has removed most of the buildings and concrete runways from these sites, new uses have been found for some of the hard standings, while sections of the perimeter taxiways survive as public roads and local farm tracks.

Wartime Exploits

When the airfield opened in November 1942, Stoney Cross was one of the Forest's larger wartime airfields. In the early months of operation Stoney Cross was home to RAF Fighter Command and construction work continued until RAF Bomber Command arrived in August 1943. The RAF handed over to the US Ninth Air Force in March 1944 and the US 367th Fighter Group attacked railways, bridges and other infrastructure targets in western France. Later they deployed on ground attack missions in support of the First Army. The Group flew a total of 55 missions from Stoney Cross, losing 21 aircraft before transferring to nearby RAF Ibsley in early July.

Meanwhile, the US 387th Bombardment Group were moving in. They began operations in late June 1944, with raids along the Normandy coast and attacks on infrastructure targets in support of ground forces. The Group left at the beginning of September and handed back to RAF Transport Command, which was busy recovering and repairing gliders used in the Normandy invasion.

Stoney Cross was on active service until the end of the war, after which the airfield played a leading role in RAF transport links with the Far East. Following closure in 1948 the airfield stood empty until the 1960s, when the runways were broken up for hardcore and most of the buildings removed. The main runway now forms the road towards Linwood and the eastern perimeter taxiway was incorporated into the road from Stoney Cross to Fritham. The steel water tower was finally demolished in 2004.

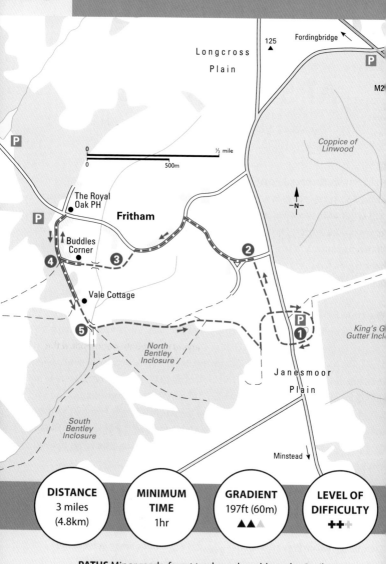

Longcross
Plain

Fordingbridge

125

M2

Coppice of
Linwood

½ mile

500m

The Royal
Oak PH

Fritham

Buddles
Corner

North
Bentley
Inclosure

King's G
Gutter Incle

Vale Cottage

Janesmoor

Plain

South
Bentley
Inclosure

Minstead

DISTANCE
3 miles
(4.8km)

**MINIMUM
TIME**
1hr

GRADIENT
197ft (60m)
▲▲▲

**LEVEL OF
DIFFICULTY**
✚✚✚

PATHS Minor roads, forest tracks and muddy paths, 2 stiles
LANDSCAPE Grazing fields, woods and heath
SUGGESTED MAP OS Explorer OL22 New Forest
START/FINISH Grid reference: SU 247135
DOG FRIENDLINESS Keep on the lead near grazing animals
PARKING Janesmoor Pond car park
PUBLIC TOILETS None on route

WALK 29 DIRECTIONS

❶ From the car park entrance, cross the road and turn right along the wide grass verge. Cross a concrete track and veer left away from the road until you reach the lane crossing your path.

❷ Turn left, follow the lane to a T-junction and turn left along the 'no through road'. Continue for 130yds (119m) past the phone box and fork left through the kissing gate onto the signposted footpath. Follow the right-hand hedge through two more kissing gates until the hedge bears away right.

❸ Cross the stile, continue along the short enclosed path and turn left over a second stile. Head for the field gate in the far corner of the paddock, then keep ahead up the hedged green lane. Go through the gate at Buddles Corner and keep ahead onto the gravel track that curves to a metalled lane.

❹ Turn right to visit the Royal Oak, then retrace your steps and keep ahead past this junction. Follow the gravelled track past the wooden barrier at Vale Cottage to a footbridge over the stream.

❺ Cross over and keep ahead up the slope into the trees. Soon there are wire fences on both sides and the path slowly matures into a track that continues as a concrete road. Follow the road to a T-junction, turn sharp left onto the former perimeter taxiway, then follow it around to the right to return to the car park.

🍴 EATING AND DRINKING

Walkers and cyclists flock to the Royal Oak, which well deserves its reputation for simple, substantial and wholesome bar food and well-kept ales. There's a vast log fire in winter and a rambling forest garden.

🥾 ON THE WALK

Right at the start of this route you'll be walking beside the former north–south runway. Once you get your eye in it's easy to pick out the straight lines of bushes fringing the poor quality turf that still struggles to grow half a century after the concrete was broken up. The last stretch of the walk follows one of the remaining concrete dispersal taxiways and leads out onto the former perimeter taxiway.

🌿 IN THE AREA

Drive down the airfield's former main runway and turn left at the T-junction to reach the Canadian Memorial at Bolderwood. Canadian Army troops stationed in the New Forest during the Second World War said daily prayers at this wooden cross from April 1944 until their departure on D-Day two months later. It now stands to the memory of those killed in action.

CASTLEMAN'S CORKSCREW

Discover how the railways
changed the New Forest.

Motorists looking at their maps in the traffic queues around Lyndhurst might well wonder why on earth the railway took so much trouble to avoid the capital of the New Forest. Between Ashurst and Brockenhurst the line loops through remote countryside, when a significantly shorter route could have given Lyndhurst a station and generated some worthwhile revenue.

Deviation and Hesitation

The railway reached Southampton in 1839 and five years later the Wimborne solicitor Charles Castleman proposed extending the line to Dorchester. Naturally enough, his railway would pass through Wimborne; but, even allowing for that, he could hardly have chosen a more roundabout route. Several of the stations were somewhat optimistically named, with Lyndhurst Road (now Ashurst), Beaulieu Road and Christchurch Road (later Holmsley) each being several miles from the places they pretended to serve. The reasons for this meandering route are unclear but soon after the line opened in 1847 it was nicknamed 'Castleman's Corkscrew'.

For many years, Holmsley was little more than a rural backwater. But the outbreak of the Second World War generated enormous demand for air power and in 1942 construction work started on a major RAF airfield at Holmsley South, little more than 1 mile (1.6km) from the railway. Holmsley Station was ideally placed to serve the new airbase, which generated vast amounts of passenger and freight traffic.

It was the silver lining in Holmsley's cloud; but, after the war, the notorious Beeching Report in 1963 proposed closing roughly a third of Britain's railways. The following year the line from Brockenhurst to Ringwood was axed. Holmsley Station had seen its last passenger.

More recently, much of the old line has been opened up to walkers and cyclists and this route follows the delightful section just west of Holmsley. You'll get great views of the heathland south of Burley from your vantage point on the old embankment, which offers a fast, level and well-drained route through this boggy valley.

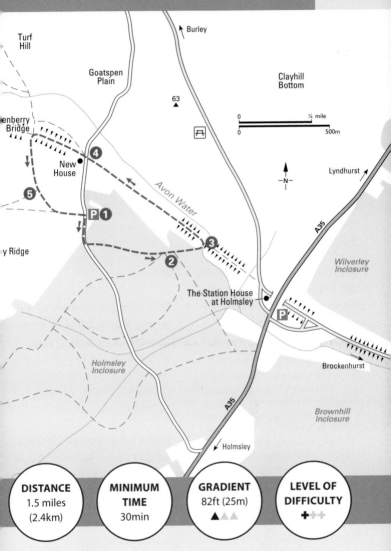

DISTANCE
1.5 miles
(2.4km)

MINIMUM TIME
30min

GRADIENT
82ft (25m)
▲▲ ▲

LEVEL OF DIFFICULTY
✚ ✚ ✚

PATHS Heathland and muddy woodland tracks, old railway path
LANDSCAPE Mixed woodland and lowland heath
SUGGESTED MAP OS Explorer OL22 New Forest
START/FINISH Grid reference: SU 221011
DOG FRIENDLINESS Can generally run free
PARKING Holmsley car park
PUBLIC TOILETS None on route

WALK 30 DIRECTIONS

❶ Turn left out of the car park and follow the lane up the hill. Cross the cattle grid and, 30yds (27m) further on, turn left through the gate into the woods. Walk down the hill and bear left at the junction to a gate.

❷ Keep ahead through the gate, follow the low causeway through the boggy woodland and climb up onto the embankment beside an old railway bridge.

❸ You can take a short diversion here by turning right to the Station House tea rooms. Otherwise, to stay on the route, turn left and follow the wide, tree-lined embankment to the former level crossing.

🍴 EATING AND DRINKING

Whether you drive or go on foot, don't miss the Station House at Holmsley. The old station buildings have been given a new lease of life as a restaurant and tea room, with railway ephemera to help set the scene. The menu covers breakfast, lunch and afternoon tea, served indoors or in the attractive patio garden.

⚓ ON THE WALK

Although most of the railway infrastructure is long gone, you can still spot some concrete fence posts at the foot of the embankment. These are typical of a wide range of pre-cast concrete items produced at the Southern Railway's Exmouth works between the wars; other examples, including loading gauges, gravel bins and footbridges, were widely distributed across the network.

❹ Cross the lane beside the striking modern house and continue through the cutting to the broken remains of Greenberry Bridge. Turn left between the abutments, fork left and follow the rough track up the hillside to a second fork.

❺ Keep left and walk towards the red-brick cottage, as far as a crossways with a gravel track. Turn left and follow the track out past a wooden barrier to the lane you walked up earlier. Turn left again and walk the short distance back to the car park.

🌿 IN THE AREA

Nearby Burley is one of the New Forest's iconic villages. Bustling with individual shops and places to eat, you'll find everything from a New Forest ice cream and bike hire to antiques and witchcraft souvenirs. New Forest Cider is made and sold at Littlemead in Pound Lane and you can watch steam-driven cider presses in action at the annual October open weekend.

BREAMORE AND THE MIZ MAZE

Explore a classic Avon Valley estate
and its ancient and mysterious maze.

Breamore, pronounced 'Bremmer', is a truly ancient village. Stretching
across the lush water-meadows and up the western chalk slopes of the Avon
Valley, it is one of Hampshire's most impressive villages. Knots of 17th-
century brick cottages and farmhouses, mostly thatched and timber-framed,
are dotted around the large boggy common that lies close to Breamore's
centrepiece, the fine Elizabethan manor house. You'll see all the main village
attractions on this walk – the manor, the Saxon church and the Countryside
Museum – as well as the mystical Miz Maze.

A Rare Survivor

Looking across the valley as you walk towards the church is the site of the
Battle of Charford AD 54. The Church of St Mary, close to Breamore House, is
a rare Saxon survivor that was built about AD980. Despite later alterations,
including a Norman porch and a 14th-century chancel, it still preserves much
of the original Saxon fabric. Note the extensive use of flints and some Roman
bricks in its construction, small double-splayed windows, an Anglo-Saxon
inscription and a magnificent Saxon stone rood above the nave doorway.
There's so much of interest here that it's worth picking up a copy of the
guidebook before you explore.

From Priory to Manor House

The pre-Reformation church was closely linked with Breamore Priory,
which once stood beside the River Avon just to the north of Breamore Mill.
Following the dissolution of the priory in 1536, Queen Elizabeth's Treasurer,
William Doddington, built the manor house from red brick in the classic
Elizabethan 'E' shape in 1583. The house is open during the summer but you'll
get a good view of the outside as you pass it at the start of your walk.

The origins of the Miz Maze are the stuff of legend. One story associates
it with the monks of Breamore Priory, who had to crawl around the maze on
their hands and knees as a penance. The circular maze is about 85ft (26m) in
diameter and formed of 11 concentric rings.

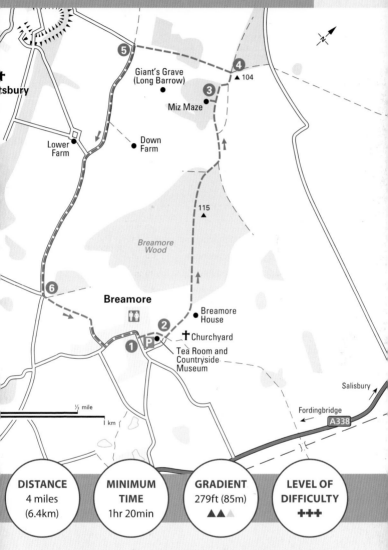

Giant's Grave
(Long Barrow)

Miz Maze

▲ 104

...sbury

Lower
Farm

Down
Farm

115 ▲

*Breamore
Wood*

Breamore

Breamore
House

✝ Churchyard

Tea Room and
Countryside
Museum

Salisbury

Fordingbridge

A338

½ mile

1 km

DISTANCE	MINIMUM TIME	GRADIENT	LEVEL OF DIFFICULTY
4 miles (6.4km)	1hr 20min	279ft (85m) ▲▲▲	+++

PATHS Country tracks, field paths and short sections of road, 3 stiles
LANDSCAPE Woodland and rolling farmland
SUGGESTED MAPS OS Explorer OL22 New Forest, OS Explorer 130 Salisbury
& Stonehenge **START/FINISH** Grid reference: SU 151187 (on Explorer OL22)
DOG FRIENDLINESS Keep under control at all times
PARKING Car park near Breamore House and Countryside Museum
PUBLIC TOILETS Opposite Countryside Museum (when house is open)

Opposite: View down from the edge of Breamore Wood

WALK 31 DIRECTIONS

❶ Walk past the tea room and Countryside Museum and turn right beside the parkland wall. Keep ahead at the drive to Breamore House for a short diversion to see the church; otherwise, turn left between the gate pillars and follow the bridleway up the drive towards the house.

❷ Pass the house and keep ahead, leaving the stables on your right as you ascend the track into Breamore Wood. Keep to the main path as it curves right, then left (by a fingerpost) on leaving the trees. Bear left at a fork on the edge of rough grassland and keep ahead along a permissive path as far as the sign to the Miz Maze.

❸ Turn left into the hilltop yew grove to find the Miz Maze, then leave the copse and turn left along the grassy swathe back down to the bridleway. Turn left and continue for 100yds (91m) to a waymarked stile beside a gate.

❹ Turn left over the stile and walk down the left-hand field-edge. Keep ahead as the path joins a track through woodland and continue past a metal barn, now walking along the woodland edge and down the side of the next field to a stile.

❺ Turn left on to the bridleway, which soon merges with a gravelled track. Pass a gate and keep ahead past the turning to Down Farm on your left. Continue past Lower Farm on your right, until you reach a metalled lane.

> **⚘ ON THE WALK**
> Not far from the Miz Maze you'll see the Giant's Grave, one of several neolithic long barrows or burial mounds on Breamore Down.

❻ Turn left here on to a bridleway, then fork right onto a signposted path, heading diagonally across a field. Crest the brow of the hill and continue towards a thatched cottage, then cross a stile and turn right onto a metalled lane. Turn left at the bottom and follow the lane back to the car park.

> **🍴 EATING AND DRINKING**
> Light lunches and afternoon tea are served at the Tea Room from noon (Easter–September when the house is open). Alternatively, call in at the Horse and Groom at Woodgreen or the Bat and Ball in Breamore.

> **❷ IN THE AREA**
> Don't miss the Countryside Museum at Breamore as it provides a fascinating insight into the days when a village was self-sufficient. You can see re-creations of village buildings and workshops, including a farm worker's cottage and a dairy and view a vast collection of agricultural machinery and tractors.

HEATH AND HOME

Experience a range of scenery as this
short walk encircles Frogham village.

When William the Conqueror established the New Forest in 1079 it was a royal
hunting ground. Royal forests were ruthlessly governed by their own legal
code and poaching or disturbing the deer was strictly forbidden. In addition,
the locals could no longer fence or enclose their land and were not allowed
to take timber or firewood from the forest. Penalties were severe and the new
regime ended a way of life that had existed up until the Norman Conquest.

Not surprisingly, there was fierce opposition and eventually the King
granted a number of concessions that were held jointly – or in common – by
the peasants. More than 900 years later, those concessions form the basis of
the 'commoning' system still practised by some 500 New Forest residents.
Between them, the 'commoners' graze about 7,000 ponies, cattle and
donkeys on the open forest and pigs are turned out in the autumn to forage
for acorns and beech mast. This ancient system plays an important part in
preserving the characteristic open heaths like those that you'll see on this
walk. Left ungrazed, these would quickly revert to scrub and woodland.

Growth of a Village

In the 18th and 19th centuries small, scattered settlements like Frogham
began to encroach on the edge of the commons. Although the village was
first recorded early in the 14th century, it wasn't large enough to support its
own church until the Congregational chapel was built in 1883. Even then,
Frogham was no more than 'a collection of rough rude huts' and the chapel
doubled up as the village school. Look behind you as you cross the road near
the start of the walk to see the little brick and slate building with its tall lancet
windows and gabled porch.

Even after the Second World War, Frogham still had its bohemian side. The
traveller and herbalist Juliette de Bairacli Levy wrote *Wanderers in the New
Forest* while living with her children in a tiny cottage close to Abbots Well.
Stories of the local gypsies dominate her book, which also describes some of
the old commoners and contemporary farming practices, such as harvesting
bracken, which have now died out.

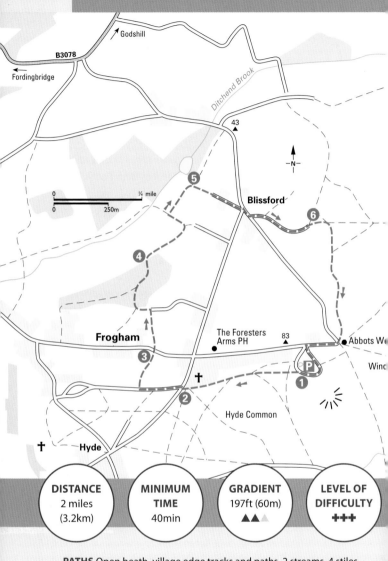

Ditchend Brook

43 ▲

—N—

5

Blissford

6

¼ mile

250m

4

Frogham

The Foresters
Arms PH

83 ▲

● Abbots W

Winc

3

P

1

†

2

Hyde Common

† **Hyde**

DISTANCE
2 miles
(3.2km)

**MINIMUM
TIME**
40min

GRADIENT
197ft (60m)
▲▲▲

**LEVEL OF
DIFFICULTY**
+++

PATHS Open heath, village edge tracks and paths, 2 streams, 4 stiles
LANDSCAPE Wide open heaths and small woods surrounding village
SUGGESTED MAP OS Explorer OL22 New Forest
START/FINISH Grid reference: SU 177128
DOG FRIENDLINESS Keep under close control on heath and on lead through
horse paddocks **PARKING** Abbots Well car park
PUBLIC TOILETS None on route

WALK 32 DIRECTIONS

❶ Walk through to the upper car park and turn right, passing the pond on your right and following the faint path across the heath, roughly parallel with the village edge. The path matures into a gravel track as you pass the outlying cottages on your left; bear right and follow the track past houses on your right to reach the road.

❷ Dodge right and left across the road, continuing down the gravel track opposite for 180yds (165m) to a kissing gate. Turn right through the gate and walk through the paddock to the kissing gate on the far side. Continue along the enclosed path to the kissing gate at the road.

🐾 EATING AND DRINKING

Donkeys cluster around the front of the Foresters Arms, so be sure to shut the gate as you go in. Inside the flagstoned bar, - ales accompany a menu that ranges from substantial sandwiches and ploughman's to jacket potatoes and daily specials. Dogs are welcomed.

---

❸ Cross the road, nip over the stile and continue to a second stile. Turn left and follow the enclosed path as it winds past a stile on your left and bears right beside a wire fence. Follow the fence through light woodland until it bends left and drops to a kissing gate at the edge of the trees.

🐾 ON THE WALK

The springs at Abbots Well were first recorded in 1215 and their water is said to be the finest in the New Forest. Sadly, the two outlets – an open one for animals and a covered chamber for people – are rather neglected in these days of piped mains water.

---

❹ Turn right, go through another kissing gate and bear left through the next paddock to a gate in the far left-hand corner. Turn right across the plank bridge just beyond the gate, cross the stile and continue through the light woodland to a stile and junction of paths.

❺ Turn right and follow the path through a gate and up the track to Abbotswell Road. Keep ahead past the junction with Blissford Hill, then turn left through the gate onto the signposted bridleway. Follow this track as it climbs to a gate at Forest Heights.

❻ Keep ahead briefly past the trees, then turn right across the open heath and follow the faint track downhill, walking roughly parallel with Abbotswell Road on your right. Jump across the tiny stream and take the clear path ahead, jumping a second stream before heading up the grassy slope to rejoin the road at the bend by the Abbots Well spring. Bear right and follow the road uphill to the car park.

DEATHLY DRAMA AT MOYLES COURT

Events that changed the course of British history were played out in this peaceful countryside.

Somewhat ironically, the turbulent days of the Monmouth Rebellion and Judge Jeffreys' Bloody Assizes are the focus of this gloriously peaceful walk. But first, a little context.

Monmouth's Rebellion

When Charles II died on 6th February, 1685, following a fit four days earlier, a shadow hung over the succession of the throne. Despite fathering at least a dozen children illegitimately, Charles and his queen remained childless. In the absence of any legitimate children, his unpopular Roman Catholic brother was proclaimed James II of England and James VII of Scotland.

In the meantime the Protestant Duke of Monmouth, the eldest of Charles' illegitimate children, was living in exile in the Netherlands and raising support for his claim to the English throne. Hearing of his father's death and James' accession, he sailed for England with his supporters, landing at Lyme Regis on 11th June. After some adventures and skirmishes in the West Country, Monmouth was pushed back onto the Somerset Levels and finally defeated by a Royalist army at the Battle of Sedgemoor on 6th July.

A Local Tragedy

Monmouth's supporters scattered and in the aftermath of Sedgemoor, the notorious Judge Jeffreys rounded up fugitives from Monmouth's army for trial in his Bloody Assizes. Two of them, Richard Nelthorpe and the Nonconformist minister John Hickes, arrived at Dame Alice's door in Moyles Court on 20th July and were given shelter for the night. But the following morning the two men were arrested along with Dame Alice who, despite her denials that the men were in her house, was tried in Winchester and convicted of treason for harbouring the King's enemies. Jeffreys sentenced her to be burned at the stake – though, following pleas for clemency, James II commuted her sentence to beheading.

Dame Alice Lisle was executed in the Square at Winchester in September 1685 and is buried beside the porch at Ellingham church.

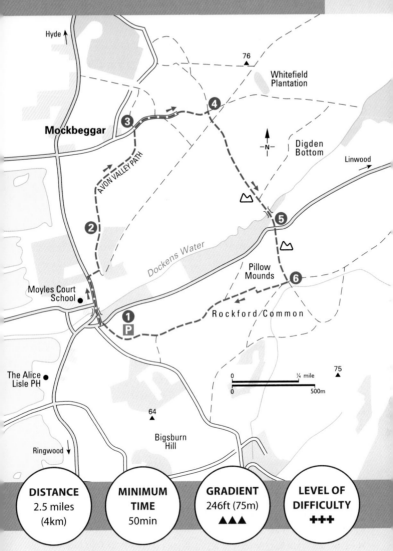

DISTANCE	MINIMUM TIME	GRADIENT	LEVEL OF DIFFICULTY
2.5 miles (4km)	50min	246ft (75m) ▲▲▲	+++

PATHS Mostly firm paths and tracks but with one very boggy area

LANDSCAPE Light woodland and forest heaths

SUGGESTED MAP OS Explorer OL22 New Forest

START/FINISH Grid reference: SU 164082

DOG FRIENDLINESS Keep under close control, especially near livestock

PARKING National Trust Rockford Common car park

PUBLIC TOILETS None on route

WALK 33 DIRECTIONS

1 Walk back down the car park access road, cross the ford and follow the road for 150yds (137m) past Moyles Court School. Turn right through the kissing gate onto the Avon Valley Path (AVP), walk up between the paddocks and turn left, continuing beside the woods to a kissing gate.

2 Keep ahead, following the waymarked AVP as it follows the contour around the hillside and bears right, with more paddocks opening up beyond the fence on your left. At the end of the paddocks, turn left at a short, stubby AVP waymark post and follow the signposted route across a boardwalk and plank bridge to a track.

3 Leave the AVP here and turn right along the track, climbing steadily past a wooden barrier and following the track up onto the open heath. As the track levels off, look out for a pond down the slope on your left.

4 Turn right here taking the clear path through the heather. Continue as the

> ### 🐾 ON THE WALK
> Rabbits have not always been as common as they are now and in earlier times were prized for their meat. Pillow mounds like the ones on Rockford Common are actually artificial rabbit warrens built from a low pile of stones and covered with soil. They probably date from late medieval times.

path drops steeply off the plateau, then pick your way through the boggy area and the footbridge to a road.

5 Cross straight over and climb steeply, staying with the path as it levels out and dives through a narrow belt of silver birch trees to a wider gravel path immediately beyond the trees.

6 Turn right and keep right at the fork a few paces further on. From here, follow the clear, level route past the old workings on your left until it joins an old metalled access road and drops down past a barrier to the car park.

> ### 🍴 EATING AND DRINKING
> Leather settees and oak beams set a relaxing tone at the iconic Alice Lisle pub on Rockford Green. Open all day for Fuller's and Gales ales, the menu features sandwiches as well as main meals. Dogs on leads are welcome in the bar or in the large garden, where there's also a play area.

> ### 🐦 IN THE AREA
> Drop in on Liberty's Owl, Raptor & Reptile Centre, just a few minutes' drive south of Ringwood. There's a large collection of birds of prey, with daily flying demonstrations featuring hawks, vultures and falcons as well as owls. Daily reptile shows also take place with snakes, lizards and spiders during the school summer holidays.

AROUND ROMAN ROCKBOURNE

Roman discoveries link Rockbourne
and Whitsbury, close to the Wiltshire border.

Pevsner claims that the village street in Rockbourne is one of the prettiest in Hampshire. This is certainly true, for the long, gently winding street is lined with Tudor and Georgian houses as well as thatched cottages.

By far the oldest known homestead is the Roman villa, discovered south of the village by a farmer in 1942. He unearthed oyster shells and tiles and the significance of the find was recognised by local antiquarian A T Morley Hewitt, whose first excavation revealed a mosaic floor. In 1956, after Morley Hewitt had bought the land, a full-scale excavation began and it was realised that the Rockbourne site was to be one of the most interesting Roman villa complexes to be discovered in the country.

Roman Legacy

In the countryside, notably in southern England where the soils were fertile, the Romans established prosperous farm estates with a villa at the centre. Villa architecture changed over the 400 years of Roman occupation. Simple circular houses were modified with the addition of wings, corridors, verandas and courtyards and housed heated bath suites and various farming activities.

Excavations at Rockbourne identified more than 70 rooms, including the pre-Roman circular hut and bathouses. A treasure trove of Roman remains were also uncovered, in particular mosaics with geometric patterning, hoards of coins, elaborate ironwork, intricate jewellery and shards of pottery with graffiti ranging from a simple symbol to a string of letters. Morley Hewitt's detailed study of the site has revealed much about the everyday life of the Roman Britons at Rockbourne. The excavations have been filled in for their own protection but you can see the outlines of the rooms and buildings marked out in the grass, the hypocaust heating systems and some mosaics.

The walk takes in the neighbouring village of Whitsbury, where the foundations of a Roman building containing a hypocaust and New Forest pottery of the 2nd and 3rd centuries AD, were found in a field between the church and Glebe House. There is also evidence of even earlier habitation and by Whitsbury Stud there is a fine example of a fortified Iron Age camp.

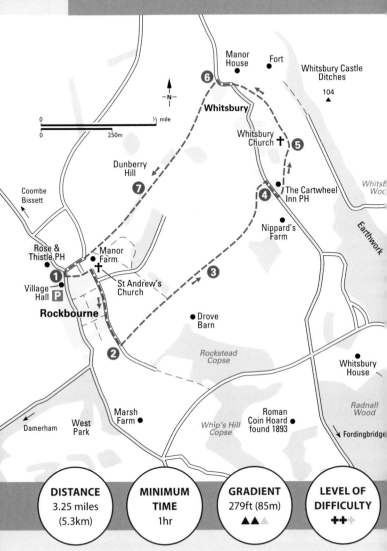

DISTANCE	MINIMUM TIME	GRADIENT	LEVEL OF DIFFICULTY
3.25 miles (5.3km)	1hr	279ft (85m) ▲▲△	++

PATHS Field paths and country tracks (may be muddy), 1 stile
LANDSCAPE Rolling arable farmland and grazing fields
SUGGESTED MAP OS Explorer OL22 New Forest
START/FINISH Grid reference: SU 113182
DOG FRIENDLINESS Under close control as far as the Cartwheel Inn; on lead
thereafter **PARKING** Rockbourne village hall car park
PUBLIC TOILETS None on route

WALK 34 DIRECTIONS

1 Cross the road from the car park, walk up the gravel drive directly opposite and follow the signposted path to the church. Keep ahead when the path doubles back into the churchyard and continue along the tree-shaded path above the houses on your right. Cross a stile and keep ahead to a metal gate.

2 Turn left and walk up the hedged green lane, then drop to a crossways in a shallow valley. Keep ahead, following the patchy hedge on your right to the far corner of the field.

🍴 EATING AND DRINKING

The Rose and Thistle in Rockbourne is a thatched 17th-century building with an unspoiled interior. In Whitsbury, the Cartwheel is noted for its real ales, home-cooked food and peaceful garden.

---

3 Cross a track and continue ahead through the small waymarked gate, now with a wire fence on your left. Keep ahead through the kissing gate at the corner of the woods and follow the narrow enclosed path across an access drive and out to the village lane in Whitsbury.

4 Turn right, pass the Cartwheel Inn and turn immediately left up the signposted footpath. Go through the kissing gate and bear left across

---

🏛 IN THE AREA

Visit the museum at the Roman villa, which displays many of the artefacts, explains its development and describes what life would have been like on this large Roman farm.

---

the paddock towards the church. Go through the kissing gate into the churchyard, walk right around the church and leave by the gate near the east end.

5 Turn left along the track, ignore the turning on your right and follow the winding track out onto the metalled drive that skirts the wooded banks of Whitsbury fort. Turn right at the end of the drive and follow the lane around to the left as far as the right-hand bend.

6 Turn left onto the signposted bridleway, keep ahead through the big white gate and continue down the wide avenue of beech trees. Go through two gates, now following the enclosed path down through the trees to a second pair of gates.

7 Keep ahead as the bridleway leads you down through a grazing field at the foot of the shallow valley. Bear gently right when you reach the farm track near the bottom of the hill and leave the field through the small gate to the right of the farm buildings. Keep ahead down the lane and turn left in the village to return to your car.

SEA CHANGE FOR ST HELENS

Discover the forces that shaped Bembridge Harbour on this attractive seaside route.

glance at a modern map tells you little about the extraordinary landscape f St Helens and its near neighbours, Brading and Bembridge. Perhaps we hould also include Sandown in the story, for until the Middle Ages it lay at he opposite end of Brading Haven, whilst Bembridge itself was an offshore land. All that changed in 1338 with the building of Yarbridge, linking the two lands together and closing off the harbour beyond Brading. Nevertheless his was still a substantial harbour.

he French Connection

his didn't go unnoticed and the French that took advantage of this safe nchorage to invade St Helens in 1340. Sir Theobald Russell beat them back nd six years later Edward III returned the compliment when he sailed from t Helens to invade Normandy. The French tried again in July 1545 and briefly ccupied the area around Bembridge and St Helens but pressure from the ocal militia and the difficulty of supplying their army forced their withdrawal.

oliday Haven

atural coastal erosion created the present harbour entrance early in the 17th entury and by the Victorian era Bembridge was growing into a fashionable esort, with daily steamer services to Portsmouth. The railway reached rading in 1864 and ten years later Parliament authorised a branch line to embridge. The line opened in 1882 behind the long embankment from embridge to St Helens, reclaiming more than 800 acres (324ha) of Brading laven and finally ending Brading's long history as a sea port.

With St Helens now on the railway map, the Duver became home to the ewly formed Royal Isle of Wight Golf Club. This wasn't just a formal title, for he membership list included Queen Victoria's youngest daughter, Princess eatrice, as well as Edward VII. The club closed in 1961 and presented the Duver to the National Trust, which now manages the area for wildlife and ecreation. Birds like dunlin and Brent geese fly south to spend the winter ere and you may see oystercatchers and lapwings roosting at high tide.

pposite: Causeway across the former millponds

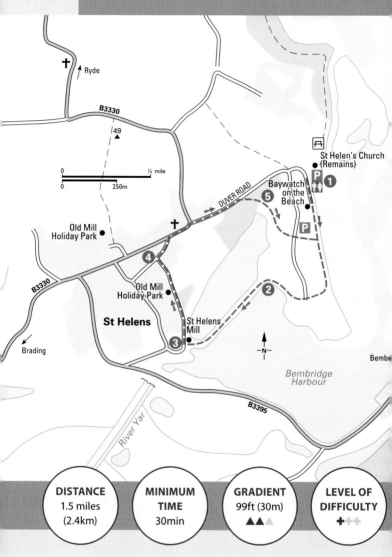

DISTANCE
1.5 miles
(2.4km)

MINIMUM
TIME
30min

GRADIENT
99ft (30m)
▲▲▲

LEVEL OF
DIFFICULTY
✚✚✚

PATHS Sea wall, firm paths, roads and grass (may be muddy)
LANDSCAPE Grazing marsh, Solent and harbour views
SUGGESTED MAP OS Explorer OL29 Isle of Wight
START/FINISH Grid reference: SZ 636894
DOG FRIENDLINESS Lead required along the roads
PARKING St Helen's (Priory Point) car park (pay-and-display)
PUBLIC TOILETS At the start (seasonal opening)

WALK 35 DIRECTIONS

❶ Face the sea wall and turn right along the beach, passing the toilets and beach café. Continue past the beach huts and turn inland, cross the boatyard access road and join footpath R86 towards St Helens. Walk beside the harbour on your left for 190yds (174m) as far as the narrow causeway on your left.

❷ Turn left and walk right across the causeway between the harbour and the former millponds on your right.

❸ Zig-zag between the buildings at the far end of the causeway and turn right past St Helens Mill, now converted as a private house. Keep ahead past the Old Mill Holiday Park and follow the lane up the hill to the green.

❹ Turn right, then right again into Uppergreen Road and fork right at the bend into Duver Road. Continue for 90yds (82m) and turn right onto footpath R88 at St Helens Common. Follow the enclosed path down beside the common and cross the footbridge onto St Helens Duver.

🍴 EATING AND DRINKING
Whether you eat indoors or on the sea wall patio, sea views come as standard at Baywatch on the Beach. Expect a good choice of sandwiches, baguettes, salads and hot main meals, with breakfast until 11.30am. There's a good children's menu, too.

❺ Keep ahead for 65yds (59m),then, when the path curves right, branch off left across the grass towards the houses on the skyline. Cross the lane and keep ahead past the car park steps on your left, then squeeze through the gap in the bushes onto the sea wall. Turn left and re-trace your steps to the car park.

🥾 ON THE WALK
You can hardly miss the tower of old St Helen's Church at the beginning of this walk. Dating from the early 13th century, the church eventually became unsafe and in 1717 a new church was built further inland. A storm destroyed the original church in 1720 and the tower was converted into the white-painted seamark that you'll see today.

🔍 IN THE AREA
Don't miss the iconic Bembridge Windmill (open March to October), given to the National Trust in 1961 by Mrs Smith of Mill Farm. Now the Island's only surviving windmill, it dates from about 1700 and was in use until just before the First World War. You can still see most of the original machinery, spread out over four floors.

WOODS AND WHISTLES AT WOOTTON

Take this history trail through wildlife-rich ancient woodlands to the Island's own steam railway.

Dividing Wootton Creek from the placid waters of the old Mill Pond, Wootton Bridge is a charming spot. Your route leads quickly away from the bustling main street, passing through farmland and quiet woodlands that are numbered among England's finest wildlife sites.

You'll pass through Hurst Copse soon after leaving the village. Parts of the copse have been planted since the area was mapped in 1793 but the remainder of these ancient woods is probably more than 400 years old and could even date from the end of the last Ice Age. Ash and English oak flourish on the rich soils running down to the Mill Pond and give shade to the lower growing hazel and field maple coppice. The woods, which also support red squirrels, dormice and eight species of bats, are protected under both UK and European wildlife laws.

A Railway Worth Preserving

As you leave the woods behind, you may hear the sound of a steam whistle heralding your first crossing of the Isle of Wight Steam Railway. Originally opened in 1875 as the Ryde and Newport Railway, there were intermediate stations serving the local communities at Wootton and Havenstreet, while the relatively isolated station at Whippingham provided for Queen Victoria's country house at Osborne. The equally grand but even more remote station at Ashey was probably built as a sweetener for Sir Henry Oglander of Nunwell House, who objected to the railway cutting through his pheasant shoot. A short branch line from Ashey also connected with the local chalk quarry until its closure in 1907, after which trains were left on the branch to serve as a grandstand for the adjacent racecourse!

Following nationalisation in 1948 the little railway was closed in 1966. But the old Ryde and Newport wasn't finished yet. Several locomotives and carriages had been saved for preservation and in 1971 the Isle of Wight Steam Railway re-opened the section between Wootton and Havenstreet. Twenty years later the heritage line was extended to Smallbrook Junction and the railway is busier than ever.

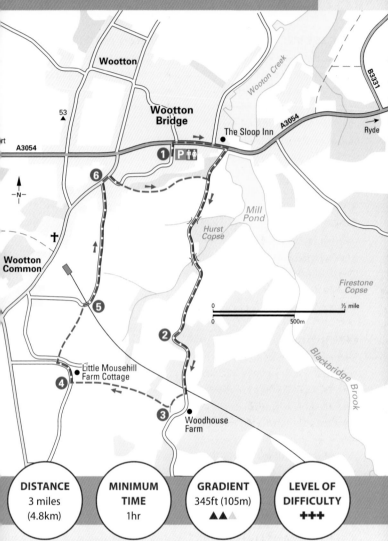

<table>
<tr><td>

DISTANCE
3 miles
(4.8km)

</td><td>

MINIMUM TIME
1hr

</td><td>

GRADIENT
345ft (105m)
▲▲▲

</td><td>

LEVEL OF DIFFICULTY
+++

</td></tr>
</table>

PATHS Mostly gravel and surfaced tracks with a short cross-field section, 6 stiles

LANDSCAPE Rolling wooded farmland

SUGGESTED MAP OS Explorer OL29 Isle of Wight

START/FINISH Grid reference: SZ 544919

DOG FRIENDLINESS Lead required across the fields between Woodhouse and Little Mousehill farms **PARKING** Brannon Way car park

PUBLIC TOILETS At the start

WALK 36 DIRECTIONS

❶ Leave the car park and turn right into Brannon Way, then right down the hill as far as the old Mill Pond. Turn right along public bridleway N1, fork right after 100yds (91m) and then left onto a gravel track at Fernhill Park. Go through the gate, follow the track past Hurst Copse and Briddlesford Parkland and continue to a T-junction.

❷ Swing left, walk through the shallow valley and climb to the railway level crossing. Keep ahead for 175yds (160m), then bear right past the entrance to Woodhouse Farm and continue for a few more paces.

❸ Turn right over the stile onto footpath N2. Bear left beside the hedge, cross a second stile and follow the tree-shaded path to a third stile. Keep ahead across the open field, jump the stile and bear left across the next field. Keep ahead after a stile, walking parallel with the hedge on your left to reach bridleway N3 at a final stile.

❹ Turn right, pass Little Mousehill Farm Cottage and follow the bridleway left at Shiloh. After 100yds (91m) turn right by the metal gates, then zig-zag right and left around the cream-washed cottage onto an attractive hedged path. Drop gently downhill, shaded by oak trees, to the railway.

> ### ⚓ ON THE WALK
>
> The ice house that you'll see on the right after passing Briddlesford Parkland was built to serve nearby Fernhill House in the late 18th century. Similar structures were common at great houses before modern refrigeration as a way of preserving winter ice for kitchen use throughout the year and about 15 of them still survive on the Isle of Wight.

❺ Go over the level crossing and dodge left at the entrance to Packsfield Farmhouse onto an enclosed path. Ignore all turnings and keep ahead as the path widens into an unmade residential lane to reach a T-junction.

❻ Turn right, then right again into Fernhill. Keep ahead into Fernside Way, then fork right onto cycle route 22 when the road bears left. Follow the well surfaced cycle track to the turning area and wooden sculpture at Fernhill Park burial ground and keep ahead down the drive. Bear left at the gate and walk back to the A3054 opposite the Sloop Inn. Now turn left and retrace your steps to the car park.

> ### 🍴 EATING AND DRINKING
>
> Beautifully located with a garden overlooking Wootton Creek, the Sloop Inn is a busy all-day enterprise that nevertheless manages to retain some character and a cosy atmosphere. Carvery is the only food option but you'll pay less for a roast than most pubs charge for a sandwich. The higher Sunday price is still excellent value.

CARISBROOKE'S CASTLE

Visit a castle with strong royal associations
and explore the surrounding countryside.

On a spur of chalk downland 150ft (46m) above the village, the grand
medieval ruin of Carisbrooke Castle stands on the site of a Roman fort. It
commands a perfect military location, overlooking the Bowcombe Valley
and the approaches to the heart of the Island.

Norman Strength and Priory Peace

The castle is probably of Saxon origin but it was the Normans who
strengthened the site with stone walls, the gatehouse and keep. The outer
bastions were built to guard against the 16th-century threat of Spanish
invasion. It was said that 'He who held Carisbrooke, held the Isle of Wight.'
For centuries the castle went hand-in-hand with the lordship of the Island,
before the Crown retained the lordship in the 16th century and appointed
a Governor of the Island, a title that continues today.

The Great Hall, which was the official residence of the Island governor
until 1944, now houses the Isle of Wight Museum. At Carisbrooke Castle
Story in the gatehouse, you'll learn more about the two occasions when it
experienced military action and find many exhibits about the castle's most
famous royal visitor, Charles I. He sought refuge here during the Civil War
in November 1647 but was imprisoned by the governor until September
1648, before being taken to London for trial and execution. He made two
unsuccessful attempts to escape and you can see the window where the
King cut the bars before he was thwarted. His children – the future Charles II,
Henry, Duke of Gloucester and 14 year-old Elizabeth (who died of pneumonia)
– were also detained here in 1650.

Leaving the castle, you'll walk through the Bowcombe Valley beside the
Lukely Brook, before returning past Froglands Farm to Carisbrooke Priory.
The Victorian Gothic buildings of St Dominic's Priory were opened in 1866 as
the home of a community of Catholic nuns. The nuns lived and worked here
until 1993, when the buildings were bought by the newly formed Carisbrooke
Priory Trust. The Trust is an independent, non-denominational charity that
holds prayers and services in the chapel every weekday at 12 noon.

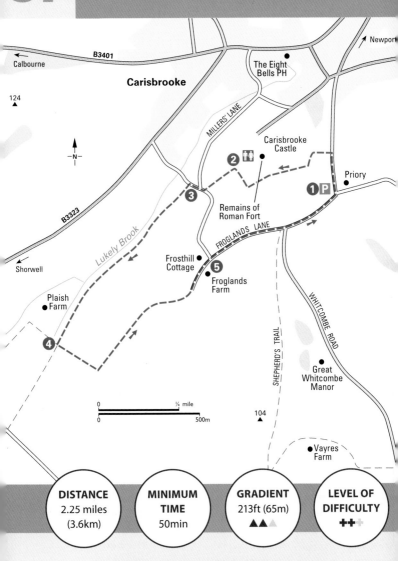

Calbourne ← B3401

Newport →

The Eight
Bells PH

Carisbrooke

124 ▲

MILLERS LANE

Carisbrooke
Castle

❷ 🚻

Priory

❶ P

B3323

❸

Remains of
Roman Fort

Lukely Brook

FROGLANDS LANE

Shorwell ↙

Frosthill
Cottage ●

❺

WHITCOMBE ROAD

Froglands
Farm ●

Plaish ●
Farm

SHEPHERD'S TRAIL

❹

Great
Whitcombe ●
Manor

0   ¼ mile
0   500m

104 ▲

Vayres ●
Farm

DISTANCE	MINIMUM TIME	GRADIENT	LEVEL OF DIFFICULTY
2.25 miles (3.6km)	50min	213ft (65m) ▲▲▲	++✛

PATHS Firm tracks, field paths and minor roads, 5 stiles
LANDSCAPE Farmland with downland views
SUGGESTED MAP OS Explorer OL29 Isle of Wight
START/FINISH Grid reference: SZ 489876
DOG FRIENDLINESS Keep dogs under control
PARKING Car park opposite Carisbrooke Priory
PUBLIC TOILETS Carisbrooke Castle and village

WALK 37 DIRECTIONS

❶ Face Carisbrooke Priory, turn left out of the car park and follow the road for 220yds (201m). Take the first footpath on the left and veer left after a few paces, climbing gently through the trees. On reaching the magnificent ruins of Carisbrooke Castle, bear left and follow the path alongside the castle walls.

❷ Turn left at the car park and follow the public footpath, signposted towards Millers Lane, until you reach Clatterford Shute. Turn right, pass Millers Lane and continue for 50yds (46m) to a stile on the left.

🕿 ON THE WALK

Crossing the meadows to Plaish Farm, you'll see a tall thin mast on the hill a few degrees to your right. This is the Rowridge transmitter, opened by the BBC in 1954 to beam 405-line television pictures to the area for the first time. UHF aerials were added in 1965 to radiate the new 625-line BBC2 channel. The mast is currently owned and operated by Arqiva, who began constructing a new mast in 2010 in readiness for the digital switchover.

✿ IN THE AREA

Visit Carisbrooke Castle (open daily), walk the battlements and savour the majestic view over the surrounding countryside. Locate the two medieval wells, one with winding gear driven by a donkey, see the Carisbrooke Castle Story in the gatehouse and discover more about the history of the island in the Isle of Wight Museum in the Great Hall.

❸ Nip over the stile and follow path N104 towards Bowcombe. Walk through the field to the next stile and keep going through the pastures, crossing two more stiles, as far as the final stile at the T-junction level with Plaish Farm.

❹ Turn left here and follow the firm, hedged bridleway N101 to a junction. Dodge right, then left and keep ahead onto the lane at Froglands Farm.

❺ Bear right at the junction by Frosthill Cottage and walk up the quiet Froglands Lane, with great views to the castle on your left. Bear left at the top of the lane and follow the roadside verge back to the car park.

🍴 EATING AND DRINKING

You'll need to pay for admission to reach the tea room at Carisbrooke Castle. Alternatively, drop down the hill to Carisbrooke High Street for breakfasts, hot lunches, sandwiches and ciabattas at Café Number 44 (closed Monday afternoons). Also in the High Street, the large family-style Eight Bells pub offers an all-day menu that includes daily specials and vegetarian options.

THE PEEPING PEPPERPOT

An invigorating walk takes in the Island's most southerly point.

The viewpoint car park high above Blackgang Chine is the ideal starting point for this intriguing ramble around the island's most southerly point, an area steeped in tales about shipwrecks, smuggling and three lighthouses. Before you lies the broad sweep of Chale Bay and high upon St Catherine's Hill to your right is a curious octagonal tower, known locally as the 'Pepperpot'. For centuries Chale Bay, in particular the treacherous rocks around Atherfield Ledge, was notorious for shipwrecks and the subsequent looting of desirable cargoes. Violent storms and huge seas drove fully-rigged sailing ships crashing against the cliffs and once as many as 14 floundered in the 'Bay of Death' on a single night.

Medieval Lighthouse

The walk begins with a long, steady climb up St Catherine's Hill to the Pepperpot and it is only here that you really realise its significance. It's all that remains of a medieval lighthouse or beacon and is, equally, a monument to the folly of Walter de Godeton. Its story begins with the wreck of a merchant ship, the *Ship of the Blessed Mary*, at Atherfield Ledge in 1313, while bound for England with a consignment of wine. The sailors escaped and sold the 174 casks of wine to the islanders, one of whom was Walter de Godeton who took 53 casks. As it belonged to a religious community in Normandy, it was considered an offence to receive the smuggled wine. Following a long trial, de Godeton was fined heavily and as an act of penance was ordered to build a pharos and oratory on the site of an earlier hermitage, so that a priest could tend the light and say prayers for those lost at sea.

The oratory has long since disappeared but the lighthouse, operational until 1638, survives as Britain's only medieval lighthouse. Close by is another partially built lighthouse known as the 'Mustard Pot'. Begun in 1785 to rekindle the St Catherine's light, the project was abandoned due to cost and the realisation that its warning light would rarely be visible due to fog. It was not until the tragic loss of the *Clarendon* in 1836 that the present lighthouse at St Catherine's Point was built.

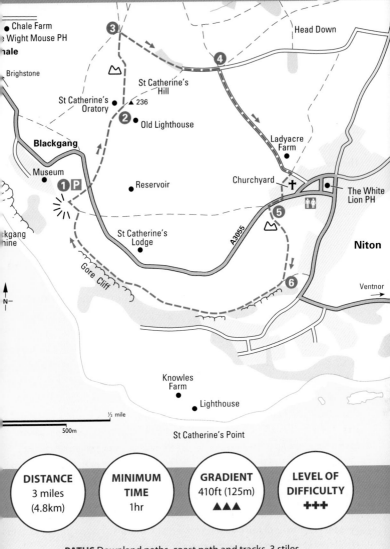

DISTANCE
3 miles
(4.8km)

MINIMUM
TIME
1hr

GRADIENT
410ft (125m)
▲▲▲

LEVEL OF
DIFFICULTY
+++

PATHS Downland paths, coast path and tracks, 3 stiles
LANDSCAPE Rolling downland and farmland, breezy cliff top
SUGGESTED MAP OS Explorer OL29 Isle of Wight
START/FINISH Grid reference: SZ 490767
DOG FRIENDLINESS Keep dogs under control at all times
PARKING Viewpoint car park above Blackgang Chine
PUBLIC TOILETS Niton (opposite the church)

WALK 38 DIRECTIONS

❶ Cross the road from the car park and climb the steps to a gate. Bear left along footpath C36 towards Gore Down and climb steadily up the grassy downland to the stile near the summit of the hill.

❷ Walk up to the old Pepperpot lighthouse. Ignore the stile by the trig point just beyond. Then, keeping the fence on your right, continue downhill to the gate in the fence near the foot of the steep slope.

> ⊕ **EATING AND DRINKING**
> During the summer and at weekends you may find an ice cream van in the car park. The White Lion in Niton, once the haunt of local smugglers, serves a varied menu and real ale. After the walk, retire to the Wight Mouse Inn in Chale for good food.

❸ Turn right through the gate and follow the grassy bridleway as it follows the contour around the flank of St Catherine's Hill to a gate. Continue along the enclosed green lane for 275yds (251m) to a stile on your left.

❹ A few paces further on, turn right to walk along the hedged bridleway NT53. Head downhill, the path becoming metalled as it enters Niton. Just before the lane, bear right into the churchyard. (Or turn left, then first right, for the White Lion and some

> ⊘ **IN THE AREA**
> Visit St Andrew's Church in Chale. It has withstood more than five centuries of storms and there is a fine view of this wild stretch of coast from the churchyard. Among the many graves are those of the sailors who died when the *Clarendon* was pounded onto rocks in Chale Bay in 1836.

refreshments.) Keep left, leave the churchyard by a small gate and turn right alongside the A3055.

❺ Take the footpath beside the last house on the left and climb up steeply through the trees to a stile. Walk ahead across grassland to the stile and follow the left-hand field-edge to the kissing gate.

❻ Turn right along the coastal path, walk through two kissing gates and soon emerge onto the open cliff top. Remain on this narrow path close to the cliff edge for nearly 1 mile (1.6km) back to the car park.

> ⅃ **ON THE WALK**
> The massive landslides around St Catherine's Point have created an undercliff world rich in wildlife. The tumbled land of hummocks and hollows with temporary ponds are the first landfall for migratory butterflies. It is also one of the best places to watch migrating birds in spring.

NATURE RESERVE AND ANCIENT BOROUGH

Discover the creeks of Newtown Estuary
and the history of the Island's former capital.

The most ancient of the Island's boroughs, Newtown was once known as Francheville and was the Island's capital after it was laid out by the Bishop of Winchester in 1256. It soon developed into a major seaport on the Newtown River estuary, with great sailing ships dwarfing its bustling quays and a thriving trade in local salt and oysters. Its streets were designed on a grid system and their names recall the medieval merchants and craftsmen – Gold Street, Drapers Alley – although most are now only grassy lanes.

Everything changed in 1377 when the town was burned down by a combined French and Spanish raid. It was never fully rebuilt but the 'town' continued to return two MPs until the Reform Act of 1832.

The old Town Hall, a 17th-century building, stands as a monument to Newtown's past eminence. It houses an exhibition about the Ferguson's Gang, a masked group of anonymous National Trust supporters that was formed in the late 1920s. With pseudonyms like Red Biddy, Bill Stickers and The Bishop, the gang bought the dilapidated Town Hall for £5 and presented it to the Trust in 1933, later raising £1,000 to restore the building.

Wildlife Haven

Today, Newtown, which has no through traffic, is a tranquil place and best explored on foot. You can wander along the network of footpaths through the old streets and visit the beautifully restored Victorian church.

Perhaps surprisingly, the windswept salt marshes and mudflats were only created in their present form as late as 1954, following a violent winter storm that breached the sea wall. The shallow creeks and estuary are a magical area and a paradise for both birds and the birders who come to admire the abundant wildfowl and waders. Oystercatchers and redshanks probe the mudflats for morsels, a variety of ducks dabble in the shallows, nesting gulls squabble on Gull Island and both common and little terns glide gracefully through the shimmering summer air. Flocks of geese wheel overhead in winter and everywhere you'll hear the evocative bubbling call of the curlew. For a small fee you can watch the birds from well-positioned hides.

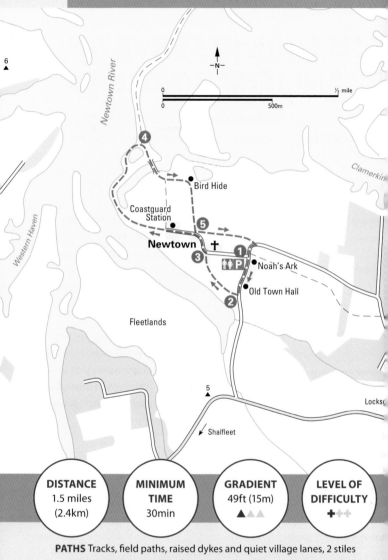

DISTANCE
1.5 miles
(2.4km)

MINIMUM TIME
30min

GRADIENT
49ft (15m)
▲▲▲

LEVEL OF DIFFICULTY
✚✚✚

PATHS Tracks, field paths, raised dykes and quiet village lanes, 2 stiles
LANDSCAPE Gently rolling farmland, salt marsh and harbour views
SUGGESTED MAP OS Explorer OL29 Isle of Wight
START/FINISH Grid reference: SZ 423905
DOG FRIENDLINESS Under close control and on lead near grazing livestock
PARKING National Trust car park opposite Newtown Town Hall
PUBLIC TOILETS National Trust toilets at the start; donation appreciated
NOTE The route includes a boardwalk that may flood at very high tides

WALK 39 DIRECTIONS

❶ Turn right out of the car park and walk down Town Lane almost to the bridge at the head of Causeway Lake.

❷ Turn right onto footpath Cb16a towards Newtown village and walk along the edge of the tidal creek to a gate, then along the edge of Hay Meadow. Keep to the path as it bears right to a gate to join a tree-lined path leading into Newtown.

🐾 ON THE WALK

Note the finely painted board or inn sign featuring the arms of the former borough above the doorway to Noah's Ark, a fine stone house close to the start in Newtown. Formerly the village inn, it is the village's oldest surviving building and surrendered its licence in 1916.

🍴 EATING AND DRINKING

The welcoming 18th-century New Inn at Shalfleet boasts flagstoned floors, a huge open fireplace and scrubbed pine tables. There's a good range of ales and an interesting menu that specialises in fresh local fish , as well as a sheltered rear garden for warm days.

---

❸ Keep ahead past the church and follow the lane left to pass a parking area. Take the path beside the Old Coastguard Station and beyond the gate keep to the left-hand edge of the meadow to reach a gate. Now follow the raised path alongside the estuary to the sheds at Newtown Quay.

❹ Head inland across the narrow wooden boardwalk to a gate. In a few paces turn left and follow the footpath towards the bird hide. Turn right at the gate and head inland to a drive and the lane.

❺ Turn left, cross the stile on your left and proceed behind the houses to a stile and lane. Turn right and walk down the lane to the old Town Hall and the car park where you began your walk.

🌿 IN THE AREA

Take a look at Shalfleet church with its impressive, fort-like tower. Built in the 11th century with 5ft (1.5m) thick walls, it was used as a refuge from French invaders during the 14th century. From here it's just a short stroll out to the small 17th-century quay, once busy with commercial traffic and now popular with yachts and sailing dinghies.

HIGH DOWN AND HEATH

Enjoy memorable views of this iconic Isle of Wight landscape.

If you enjoy razzmatazz, fairground rides and a liberal dose of shopping for souvenirs, then the Needles Park will be right up your street. From the carousel and the teacup ride to the glass studio and the sweet manufactory, there's sure to be something that takes your fancy. But don't leave Needles Park without seeing the monument to Marconi, close to the viewing platform at the far end of the park. For it was here, at the age of just 23, that the Italian-born wireless pioneer established his experimental wireless telegraphy station at the old Royal Needles Hotel in 1897.

But if your tastes are quieter or more cerebral, don't worry – there's plenty here for you, too. The bustle of Needles Park is quickly left behind and if a westerly wind doesn't take your breath away, then the scenery most certainly will. From his home at nearby Farringford, the Victorian poet laureate Alfred, Lord Tennyson, declared that the clifftop air was worth sixpence a pint and its value has certainly appreciated since then. With a clear blue sky and the wind behind you, the walk across West High Down is as close to flying as you can get without actually leaving the ground and the view across Alum Bay to the coloured cliffs is one that you won't easily forget.

Right at the start of your walk you'll see the small replica Needles lighthouse just as you leave the car park. Its full-size counterpart has stood at the western end of the Needles since 1859, when it replaced an earlier structure at the top of the Downs. The light, which stands 80ft (24m) above sea level, is visible for up to 14 miles (22.5km) and was originally tended by a resident keeper and at least two assistants. The lighthouse, however, was converted to automatic operation in 1994.

A Tunnel Above the Needles

Don't miss the Needles Old Battery, which is open daily, perched high on the cliffs above the Needles rocks. The imposing Victorian fort was built in 1862 and saw active service in both World Wars. Children will love the underground tunnel that leads out to a searchlight post and the clifftop National Trust tea room is a favourite with people of all ages.

Opposite: The sweep of sand at Alum Bay

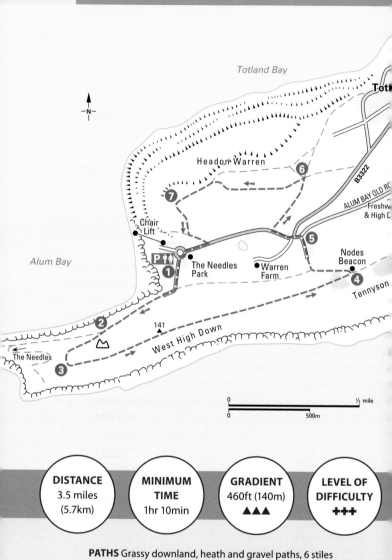

Totland Bay

Headon Warren

Chair Lift

Alum Bay

The Needles Park

Warren Farm

Nodes Beacon

Tennyson

141

West High Down

The Needles

B3322

ALUM BAY OLD RO

Freshw & High D

DISTANCE 3.5 miles (5.7km)	**MINIMUM TIME** 1hr 10min	**GRADIENT** 460ft (140m) ▲▲▲	**LEVEL OF DIFFICULTY** +++

PATHS Grassy downland, heath and gravel paths, 6 stiles
LANDSCAPE Stunning coastal clifftop scenery, heath and downland
SUGGESTED MAP OS Explorer OL29 Isle of Wight
START/FINISH Grid reference: SZ 307853
DOG FRIENDLINESS Lead required along the Old Battery access road
and near livestock **PARKING** Needles Park (charges apply)
PUBLIC TOILETS Needles Park

WALK 40 DIRECTIONS

❶ Walk up the metalled lane from the miniature lighthouse at the car park entrance, towards the Needles Old Battery. Just beyond the first bend, nip up the steps on your right for panoramic views of Alum Bay and the Solent and continue above the road for about 650yds (594m).

❷ Cross the road, turn left onto the signposted coastal path and climb steeply away from the road, over a stile and up the slopes of West High Down. Double back just before the next stile, still following the coastal path towards the summit of the Down.

❸ Turn left and follow the grassy path along the ridge, with spectacular views all the way along the south coast from Tennyson's Monument to St Catherine's Point. The gorse bushes cluster round as you drop down towards the fence that heralds the climb onto Tennyson Down.

🍴 EATING AND DRINKING

You'll find hot meals, pasties, ice creams and more, right on site at the Needles Park. For a complete contrast, light lunches and farmhouse cream teas are served in rural seclusion at Warren Farm (seasonal opening); or head to the High Down Inn for real ales and a menu that features locally sourced Isle of Wight seafood, meat and poultry.

❹ Don't cross the stile here but double back left onto the grassy path that drops downhill towards a whitewashed house in the trees ahead. As you draw level with the house, turn right over the stile and follow the enclosed path past the houses to a stile on your left. Nip across and walk down beside the hedge to a stile near the junction with Alum Bay Old Road.

❺ Turn left along the road towards Needles Old Battery for 200yds (183m), then turn right over the stile onto footpath T16 towards Headon Warren. Keep the wire fence on your left as you climb the slope to a stile, cross over into the National Trust's estate and climb 100yds (91m) to a wooden signpost.

❻ Turn left just before the signpost and walk along the path through the bushes. Views to the Needles open up as the path swings right and climbs to a junction. Turn left, passing the burial mound on your right and keep ahead along the gravel path through the heather as far as a bench seat and coastal path waymark post.

❼ Turn left and follow the coastal path downhill towards the car park. Keep left at the fork, then left at the T-junction and follow the path down to meet the B3322 at a gate. Turn right, then left and follow the coastal path back to the car park.

Walking in Safety

All these walks are suitable for any reasonably fit person, but less experienced walkers should try the easier walks first. Route finding is usually straightforward but you will find that an Ordnance Survey map is a useful addition to the route maps and descriptions.

RISKS

Although each walk here has been researched with a view to minimising the risks to the walkers who follow its route, no walk in the countryside can be considered to be completely free from risk. Walking in the outdoors will always require a degree of common sense and judgement to ensure that it is as safe as possible.

- Be particularly careful on cliff paths and in upland terrain, where the consequences of a slip can be very serious.
- Remember to check tidal conditions before walking on the seashore.
- Some sections of route are by, or cross, busy roads. Take care and remember traffic is a danger even on minor country lanes.
- Be careful around farmyard machinery and livestock, especially if you have children with you.
- Be aware of the consequences of changes in the weather and check the forecast before you set out. Carry spare clothing and a torch if you

are walking in the winter months. Remember the weather can change very quickly at any time of the year and in moorland and heathland areas, mist and fog can make route finding much harder. Don't set out in these conditions unless you are confident of your navigation skills in poor visibility. In summer remember to take account of the heat and sun; wear a hat and carry spare water.

On walks away from centres of population you should carry a whistle and survival bag. If you do have an accident requiring the emergency services, make a note of your position as accurately as possible and dial 999.

COUNTRYSIDE CODE

- Be safe, plan ahead and follow any signs.
- Leave gates and property as you find them.
- Protect plants and animals and take your litter home.
- Keep dogs under close control.
- Consider other people.

For more information on the Countryside Code visit:
www.naturalengland.org.uk/ourwork/enjoying/countrysidecode